Unlocking the Power of Your Creativity
Copyright © 2015 John W. Stanko

ISBN 978-1-63360-013-3
For Worldwide Distribution
Printed in the U.S.A.

PurposeQuest Ink
P.O. Box 8882
Pittsburgh, PA 15221-0882
412.646.2780

Table of Contents

Creativity Tips and Strategies

Introduction

When I was 57 years of age, I went back to school to earn my Doctor of Ministry degree. I did this for several reasons. The first was that the seminary where I had received a doctorate in Pastoral Ministries had failed to finalize their accreditation, leaving me with an unaccredited degree. The second was that I was teaching regularly on the topics of purpose, productivity and cognitive learning, and I wanted to do some extended study to deepen my insight in those three areas – and to make sure I wasn't teaching anything that did not have a solid biblical foundation. I felt going back to school would give me the chance and the need to study, and it did provide that much needed opportunity.

It was during the pursuit of that degree that I found myself in the opening chapters of Genesis on a regular basis. It was there that I developed what I call my theology of creativity, along with a theology of teamwork, purpose and rest. Those three will have to wait for a later book. This book shares some of what I learned about creativity during those school years.

Before Adam and Eve sinned, they had the ability to express and enjoy five things:

1. **Fellowship with God**—"And the Lord God commanded the man, "You are free to eat from any tree in the garden; but you must not eat from the tree of the knowledge of good and evil, for when you eat from it you will certainly die" (Genesis 2:16);

2. **Purpose**—"God blessed them and said to them, 'Be fruitful and increase in number; fill the earth and subdue it. Rule over the fish in the sea and the birds in the sky and over every living creature that moves on the ground'" (Genesis 1:28);

3. **Creativity**—"Now the Lord God had formed out of the ground all the wild animals and all the birds in the sky. He brought them to the man to see what he would name them; and whatever the man called each living creature, that was its name" (Genesis 2:19);

4. **Teamwork**—"The Lord God said, 'It is not good for the man to be alone. I will make a helper suitable for him'"– Genesis 2:28); and

5. **Rest**—"Then God blessed the seventh day and made it holy, because on it he rested from all the work of creating that he had done"—Genesis 2:3).

After they fell, all those things were still present and active, although they would never be the same because of their sin – never that is, until Jesus came. When Jesus came, His mission was to restore things as they were intended to be in the Garden. In other words, Jesus came to restore man's ability to have fellowship with God, flow in purpose, be creative, work in teams and truly rest from any efforts to gain God's favor. This mission was summarized in Colossians 3:18-23:

And he is the head of the body, the church; he is the beginning and the firstborn from among the dead, so that in everything he might have the supremacy. For God was pleased to have all his fullness dwell in him, and through him **to reconcile to himself all things**, whether things on earth or things in heaven, by making peace through his blood, shed on the cross.

Once you were alienated from God and were enemies in your minds because of your evil behavior. But now **he has reconciled you by Christ's physical body through death to present you holy in his sight,** without blemish and free from accusation—if you continue in your faith, established and firm, and do not move from the hope held out in the gospel. This is the gospel that you heard and that has been proclaimed to every creature under heaven, and of which I, Paul, have become a servant (emphasis added).

Jesus came to reconcile all things to God but the message of the Church historically has been that Jesus came to restore one thing: fellowship with God. The other four have been left untouched for the most part by the Church's teaching or emphasis. That has not been wrong to emphasize fellowship, it's just been incomplete. Jesus came to help you be who God intended you to be but could not be due to sin. In other words, God came to restore your creativity, along with purpose, your ability to work with teams and your capacity and need to rest.

This book contains 52 essays in Four Sections. The essays are all former Monday Memos that I have written since 2001. Over time, I have emphasized many topics in the Memos and one of them was creativity. I decided to separate and edit them, then categorize them into four areas that are pertinent to your creativity: A Theology of Creativity; Your Role in Creativity; Fear; and Strategies and Tips for Creativity. There may be an essay that could fit into more than one category and there may be some that you consider a "stretch" to be there at all. My purpose was not to make a comprehensive presentation, but to try and use what I had already written and give them some sense of order.

Notice that there are 52 entries, which means you can read one a week for a year or go through the book at your own pace, whether quickly or slowly. A few of the essays build on the previous one, but most stand alone, which means you can read them in any order you choose.

Some have homework or assignments, mostly things for you to reflect on and consider for a few days. I hope that all of them contribute to your understanding that you are a creative person by God's will and you will glorify Him as you express who you were created to be.

I have often said a bird doesn't sing because it has a contract, or is paid, or has an audience or has practiced. A bird sings because God created it to sing; it can't help but do so. The same is true for your creativity. I hope this book helps you sing your song with enthusiasm and skill and that those around you will stop what they are doing to pay attention. Even if they don't, I urge you to keep on singing whatever song God has assigned, and that you will enlist God's help in the creative process because your creativity was His idea in the first place. Thanks for reading and now let's get busy unlocking the power of your creativity.

John W. Stanko
Pittsburgh, PA
April 2015

A Theology of Creativity

In this first Section, I attempt to point out some of the things that the Bible has to say about creativity and also some of the biblical behaviors that can enhance your creativity. This Section is not meant to be an exhaustive theological study, but rather a primer or teaser to encourage more study and reflection on your part. I also attempt to show that Jesus came to restore your ability to create, having modeled a creative life while He ministered on earth. My goal is simple: to help you get comfortable with the fact that you are creative and it's God's will for you to be so.

Adam's Children

Do you consider yourself a creative person? What creative outlets do you have, or rather how many do you give yourself permission to have? For most of my adult life, I did not give myself permission to pursue creativity and I wasn't open to the fact that I am creative. My self-image was that of an administrator, and creativity and administration were at odds with one another—or so I thought.

Are you creative? If your answer is no, then perhaps you need to change the way you view creativity and, consequently, view yourself. If you are open to that possibility, then I urge you to read on.

ADAM'S ZOO

Adam was made by God to be creative and we are Adam's children. After God created Adam, He invited him to enter into the creative process by naming the animals:

> "Now the Lord God had formed out of the ground all the beasts of the field and all the birds of the air. He brought them to the man to see what he would name them; and whatever the man called each living creature, that was its name. So the man gave names to all the livestock, the birds of the air and all the beasts of the field" (Genesis 2:19-20).

Adam decided what the animals were to be called; it was an expression of his creative dominion in the Garden.

2

Too often, we have identified only musicians, songwriters, poets and writers as creative—and they are indeed creative. Those expressions, however, are only a few of the creative expressions that are available to Adam's children. Let's take a look at the essence of creativity that is part and parcel with who you are and then see if you can't get even more specific about your area(s) of creativity:

1. I don't want to be offensive, but you were made to create other human beings. When you reach maturity and marry, in most cases you must take precautions to *limit* your creativity.

2. Scientists tell us that every seven years you have a totally new set of cells in your body. Your cells are constantly dividing and creating new cells.

3. One of the first things I did when I returned home recently was to get a haircut. In most cases, your body is creating new hair, nails and whiskers on a daily basis.

4. Your body is constantly creating what it needs to carry on life. Your stomach creates gastric juices, sweat glands produce sweat and ears create wax!

5. What happens when you go to sleep? You create dreams and are a "dream machine." For every eight hours of sleep you dream for almost two. Your mind is constantly creating symbolic sleep scenarios that help you maintain your psychological equilibrium.

6. Every day you create ideas and thoughts and scenarios with you in them with daydreams.

7. You talk every day, stringing words and ideas together creatively.

YOU ARE SO CREATIVE!

I hope you get the picture. Like Adam, you are creative and God wants and needs you to express your creativity in every day life. Stop saying you aren't creative—you are! I have assembled a list of creative expressions people have sent me over the years, and it is included in the Appendix of this book and on my website. Take a look at that list and see how many expressions are present in your life and then, settle once and for all your perspective on your own creativity.

Perhaps then you will see yourself as creative, which is just how the Lord wants you to see yourself. Once you see yourself as creative, you must then give yourself permission to pursue and release creativity in ways not possible up to this point in your life.

Creativity is a War

A while back I read Julia Cameron's book *The Right to Write.* Cameron always stirs my creative juices, especially where writing is concerned. While I'm sure I do not agree with her theology, I agree with her that writing and creativity are for the most part spiritual experiences. Let's look at a few things she has to say.

WHO SAID WHAT ABOUT CREATIVITY

In one of her chapters, Cameron quoted the following artists concerning their creativity:

- *"The music of this opera (**Madame Butterfly**) was dictated to me by God. I was merely instrumental in getting it on paper and communicating it to the public"* - Giacomo Puccini.

- *"Straightaway the ideas flow in upon me, directly from God"* - Johannes Brahms.

- *"The position of the artist is humble. He is essentially a channel"* - Piet Mondrian.

- *"I myself do nothing. The Holy Spirit Himself accomplishes all through me"* - William Blake.[1]

Therefore if creativity is a spiritual expression and you are a spiritual person, why don't you create more? May I suggest three enemies that battle against your God-given ability to create.

THREE ENEMIES OF CREATIVITY

1. *Fear*. I've written and taught about fear on many occasions. How many fears can you think of that could prevent you from being creative? I can think of fear of failure, poverty, ridicule, family, culture, authority, inadequacy, and success. Can you think of any others?

If you are going to express your creativity, you must face and overcome the oppression of fear. It will paralyze your efforts and cause you to procrastinate, hoping for a more opportune time. Remember what Paul wrote his disciple Timothy: "For God has not given us a spirit of fear, but of power and of love and of a sound mind" (2 Timothy 1:7 NKJV). If you are afraid, what are you prepared to do about it?

2. *Comparison*. When you compare what you do to what others have done, it can cause you to stop being creative. In your opinion, you aren't "as good" as the other person. Stop and think about that. What is *good* where creativity is concerned? Is creativity a process and can your simple efforts today lead to stellar creativity tomorrow? Is it wise to compare your initial or mature efforts to what others may have spent a lot of time developing?

Paul described an important principle that he used when he looked at his work: "We do not dare to classify or compare ourselves with some who commend themselves. When they measure themselves by themselves and compare themselves with themselves, they are not wise" (2 Corinthians 10:12-13). Why not do something creative this week and discipline yourself *not* to compare it what anyone else has done? Is it the best it can be right now? If it is, then I would say you have done a good job.

3. *Perfectionism*. I depict the drive for perfectionism as a little old man that lives inside you, ready to criticize and disqualify what you create because it isn't good enough. That little old man is cranky and refuses to be satisfied. I know of only One who is perfect, and He is God. While you should

strive for excellence and your best performance, you can never expect it to be truly perfect.

The pursuit of perfection is unrealistic and will hinder you from doing something significant just because it isn't perfect. I can't find a verse that talks about perfectionism, but I can find one that speaks to excellence: "Whatever you do, work at it with all your heart, as working for the Lord, not for men" (Colossians 3:23). Perhaps the distinction between perfection and excellence will help you do something that you haven't done up to this point in time just because it isn't the best that anyone can do.

IT'S A WAR!

I close by again asking the question I raised earlier: If you are a spiritual person and creativity is spiritual, why don't you create more often? Perhaps it is because creativity is more of a battle than you anticipated. I hope I have helped you identify some of the enemies of your creativity and I further hope you will determine to enter into a season of creativity that begins just as soon as you finish reading this essay. Fight the good fight and express your innate creativity latent within your heart and mind as you conquer your creativity enemies.

Creator God, Creative Man

Have you ever thought about Jesus and His creativity? Jesus was a creative man. If you attribute Jesus' creativity to His divinity, you won't gain much help or understanding to assist you in your own creative endeavors. If you see, however, that Jesus was a creative *man*, then there may be things in His life to help you be more creative. You probably know what I think about this issue, but to make sure you do, you had better read on.

A TEACHING CARPENTER

Jesus was a carpenter, so He made things from wood with His hands. One second-century bishop reported wooden yokes Jesus made in the first century were still in use 100 years later! That tells us that Jesus wasn't only creative, He was committed to excellence—He did good work.

There's also a good chance that Jesus, as the oldest son, ran a carpentry business that supported more than just Himself. His brothers could have been in business with Him and that meant He also expressed His creativity by running a business, making payroll and managing inventory, accounts and customer service. He also would have supported His widowed mother from the business as well.

But Jesus' creativity didn't stop there. At the age of 30, He changed careers, starting an itinerate ministry through which He continued to express tremendous creativity. He was creative in building and equipping an effective team of men and women who traveled with Him.

When Jesus performed miracles, He did so with

flair and distinction. One time He spit on the ground, made mud and smeared it on a blind man's eyes. Another time, He put His fingers into a deaf man's ears and touched the end of the man's tongue with His spit. Jesus answered His critics with creative retorts that delighted the crowds. His insight into Scripture held people's attention for days on end as He impressed the crowd with His fresh approach to God and the Word.

Perhaps Jesus' greatest creative expression, however, was in His teaching. When He taught, He used parables—stories from everyday life that imparted truth. Where did He get those stories? He made them up. They came from His creativity, perhaps the same creativity He learned and perfected as a carpenter. Jesus used parables with lessons drawn from agriculture, business, current events, family life, and construction. He was such a creative teacher that the people would walk for days to listen to Him for days - and then have to walk home for days after it was all done. Mark reported: "The large crowd listened to him with delight" (Mark 12:37).

THE IMPLICATIONS FOR YOU

Why is this important? First of all, Jesus' creativity did not emanate from His divinity only. He was and is the Creator God but was also a creative Man. On earth He expressed His creativity as a Jewish man who observed life and saw God in all of it. Secondly, if Jesus the man was creative, then He can help you be creative. And finally, you will fulfill your purpose as you carry on the creative tradition that was modeled by the Son of God and fulfilled in the power of the Holy Spirit. You are not here to maintain; you are here to creatively advance the kingdom of God. One might argue that your creativity is how you will fulfill the mandate given to Adam and all his children to subdue the earth and rule over it.

I have an assignment for you. Take some time to read Proverbs 8. Do you see wisdom speaking there? That "wisdom" certainly sounds a lot like Jesus to me. Pray through this Proverb and then ask the Lord for creative wisdom. Ask Him to help you use the ordinary lessons of daily life, just like Jesus did, to create something extraordinary. Don't see your creativity as an exception or something that you use from time to time. See it as a powerful source of daily inspiration that will help you both fulfill your purpose and also do great things. As you understand this, I know your life will be changed as mine has been these last few years.

Week
#4

Resurrection Power

Easter isn't what it used to be. Today it is mostly about Easter bunnies, eggs, candy and mall sales. When I was a child, I can remember businesses closing down between noon and 3 PM on Good Friday and no business ever open on Easter Sunday. There was never any school on Good Friday and Easter Monday. I was in England a few years ago for Easter and I can remember thinking that, if it wasn't for the hotels advertising Easter Sunday dinner, I would never have known that Easter was even approaching.

This entry is about the good old days, but not about those of 50 years ago when I was young. The good old days I want to remember are those days 2,000 years ago when Jesus came back to life, having been dead for three days.

Easter is still one of the best-attended church days, when thousands attend Mass or service to commemorate Jesus' resurrection. Think of it: All these people come back to commemorate the fact that the Spirit brought a dead man back to life. They actually believe that it happened!

If you believe that Jesus was raised from the dead, and I hope you do, then you can believe anything! You can trust God to heal cancer because, after all, cancer is tough to overcome, but it's not as tough as death. If you believe that God raises the dead, you can believe He will help you start a business. Starting a business is hard work, but it's not as hard as raising someone back to life

It's not enough that you go to church on Easter to bear witness to the fact that Jesus is alive. You must somehow allow that fact to make a difference in your life, how you live

11

and what you expect from God. Paul referred to this when he wrote: *"And if the Spirit of him who raised Jesus from the dead is living in you, he who raised Christ from the dead will also give life to your mortal bodies through his Spirit, who lives in you" (Romans 8:11).*

The Spirit lives in you, the same Spirit that raised Christ from the dead! He is not "out there" doing good work with the same power that raises dead people. He is in you. What difference should that make when you pray, work and serve? I think it should make a big difference. Is it? Is the power of Easter Sunday present in your life and work all year long? Can you see the effects of resurrection life and power in your creativity as you overcome obstacles and express your unique insight, perspective and gifting?

If not, then think about Romans 8:11 and ask God to show you how you can allow this life-giving Spirit more room in your life in the coming days and weeks. God's Spirit is waiting to help you create, but He won't create for you. That's what you have to do, but if you believe in the Resurrection, then find ways to allow that same Spirit and Resurrection power to help you as you create.

Tell Your Story

I was studying and writing recently, when I noticed a verse in Psalm 107 that caught my attention. It's a verse you are probably familiar with, but what struck me is that the verse is an exhortation for you (and me) to publish and broadcast! You may not see it like that, but let me give you a little more background. Here is the verse: "Let the redeemed of the Lord tell their story—those he redeemed from the hand of the foe" (Psalm 107:2).

Do you have a story? I know you do, for God has done great things for you just as He has for me. That is what's known as your testimony and you are to tell it. One way is to do so in church, but in today's modern church services, where is there time to testify? That means you (and I) must find other ways to tell God's story, or your story about God. That is where publishing, social media and the like come in. If you know me, you know I don't often use social media for personal things, but I use it every day to "publish" what God is showing me and what I am learning. I do my best every day to tell my story. What about you?

After I noticed Psalm 107:2, I did more research and found two interesting things in Scripture that go along with that verse from Psalms. One is in Deuteronomy 31:19: "Now write down this song and teach it to the Israelites and have them sing it, so that it may be a witness for me against them." God instructed Moses to write a song and teach it to Israel. I had never seen that before. The nature of the song was to remind Israel of God's faithfulness in a day when they would go astray, but I had never noticed that

God commanded Moses to be creative and write music. Do you have any music in you that needs to be written? That is another way of telling your story.

The second verse I found in my study was in Joshua 18:4: Appoint three men from each tribe. I will send them out to make a survey of the land and to write a description of it, according to the inheritance of each. Then they will return to me." I had never noticed before that God commanded the spies who were sent out to submit their report in writing of what they saw in the Promised Land. Their story was not what God had done but what God was going to do when they entered the Land He was giving them. Part of your story is your faith vision of what is yet to come.

Now you have three biblical reasons to publish, write and create: 1) to tell your story of what God has done for you; 2) to remind you and others of God's faithfulness; 3) to report in faith what you see pertaining to God's purpose and plan for you that is yet to be. If you are waiting for God to send you an engraved invitation to write or be creative, it's not going to happen because He's already directed you to do so in His word. If you stop underestimating the power of what you see and what you have been through to help others, you will have even more incentive to publish and broadcast. Now that you have biblical reasons to do so as well, you should have all of the reasons that you need to express your creativity.

Creative Energy

I have written a fair share of books and always have people ask how I find time to write. Maybe you are thinking the same thing. Well, even if you were not, that is what I am going to address here, so read on to see what I have to say!

DIVINE ENERGY

I find time to write because I have tapped into divine energy. There is a formula but it's not a secret one and you can access it just like I can. The formula, if I can call it that, is found in Paul's letter to the Ephesians: "Now to him who is able to do immeasurably more than all we ask or imagine, according to his power that is at work within us, . . ." (3:20).

I have learned to rely on the power that is at work in me. It's that simple. It's at work in me and in us and that means you. If it's available to all, however, why don't more people have it? More importantly, why don't you have it?

DIVINE PURPOSE

You may not have this energy because you have not tapped into your divine purpose. And when you do and that energy is activated, you then find energy for all kinds of creative expressions. You use your time more effectively and you have the incentive to press through your fears to try new things and then keep on trying and improving.

There are a two other tips I can offer here, so let me do that before we move on:

1. I ask for wisdom when I write and create. According to James:

"If any of you lacks wisdom, you should ask God, who gives generously to all without finding fault, and it will be given to you. But when you ask, you must believe and not doubt, because the one who doubts is like a wave of the sea, blown and tossed by the wind. That person should not expect to receive anything from the Lord. Such a person is double-minded and unstable in all they do" (1:5-8).

2. I remember what Proverbs teaches and that is that wisdom is basically understanding of how to do new things in fresh ways (or old things in fresh ways):

"I [wisdom] was there when he set the heavens in place, when he marked out the horizon on the face of the deep, when he established the clouds above and fixed securely the fountains of the deep, when he gave the sea its boundary so the waters would not overstep his command, and when he marked out the foundations of the earth. Then I was constantly at his side. I was filled with delight day after day, rejoicing always in his presence, rejoicing in his whole world and delighting in mankind" (Proverbs 8:27-31).

I figure if wisdom could help shape the earth and all of creation, then it can help me write my books or daily devotionals. All I have to do is ask and believe, as long as I am connected to my purpose activities. This week, why not ask for wisdom and believe that you have received it? Stop fighting what you have been considering and take steps to do it. While you do that, I will be writing every day, trusting that God is answering my prayer for wisdom to write, which releases my creative energy.

Living Water

One of the terms I heard repeatedly when I was earning accreditation to facilitate a cognitive learning seminar was "free flow." Free flow is when one doesn't have to consciously think about how to act or behave, one just does it. That caused me to think about something that Jesus said: "Whoever believes in me, as the Scripture has said, streams of living water will *flow* from within him" (John 7:38). I got to thinking about this flow and how it relates to the flow I am studying. Here are some thoughts and questions I continually ask myself:

1. **My faith in Jesus should produce something that comes out from my innermost man.** Is my faith active or stagnant? Do I have productive faith or is it doctrinal, narrow and legalistic? Is it touching others or limited to my use and benefit?

2. **Streams have direction.** Do I know where I am going and what I want to do? Am I able to carry others in the strength of my current?

3. **Streams have flow.** There is a constancy of movement with a steady supply of water. Is my creativity pouring forth? Is there an increasing amount of water coming forth from me as my faith and confidence increase?

4. **The water is living water, able to support**

other life. Is my life sustaining life in others? Do people touch me and feel that their lives have improved?

5. **The conditions of drinkable water that can sustain life are clarity, taste and purity**. Is my life transparent—am I sharing my stories and lessons with others? How is my taste? Does my water taste like me? Is it bitter or salty or pure? Is it free from the pollution of greed, self-promotion and exaggeration?

When I think about flow, I think of how the gospels were written. God was directing and inspiring the authors, but they were using the vocabulary, sentence structure and experiences that were unique to them. They were in the flow as they wrote, free to be themselves, yet all the while God was using them for a great purpose. I am not equating yours or my free flow with the creation of God's inspired Word, but the process is similar. I don't want to dam up what God has put inside me while He uses me just as I am, just as He created me to be.

How about you? Are you happy with your flow right now? If so, what can you do to increase your current? If not, what can you do to find your flow? These are important things to think about and free flow is s worthy goal if you are going to find a creative flow that is true to who you are, to who God made you to be.

When the Truth Doesn't Set You Free

There isn't a week that goes by where I don't quote John 8:32 to someone, "You will know the truth and the truth will set you free." Why is this such an important passage? Often you are holding onto a truth that you think is the truth but in reality is a half-truth or non-truth. It isn't freeing but preventing you from being or doing all that you could. When we accept this adjusted and real truth, it will set you free.

In Jesus' day, the Jews held the "truth" that no prophet could come from Galilee or no good from Nazareth. Thus they missed the truth of Jesus because they held some other "truth." The first Jewish believers knew the truth that everyone had to follow the law of Moses even after they professed faith in Christ. Thus they missed the freedom that came from putting their total trust in Jesus.

We could go on and on about the "truths" that have bound whole cultures. At one point, we "knew" that the world was flat, the sun orbited the earth, that people with lighter skin were superior to those with darker, and that bleeding someone who was sick would make them well. Men and women were ready to, and often did, die for these so-called truths. Sincerely holding that a belief is true isn't the issue, for I can be sincere and that only makes me sincerely wrong.

What truth are you holding about yourself that isn't setting you free, but limiting your effectiveness? Are you thinking, "I'm too old," "I'm too young," "I'm not that talented," "I can't get my hands on that kind of money to start my business," or "I can't write"? If you are, is that the truth or is it a lie that appears to be or sounds like truth? Are you part of an organization that believes the same kind of limiting "truths"?

I was on the road not too long ago and awoke at 3 AM. I couldn't sleep because I was examining some truths that I've held about myself that weren't true at all. They limited me and put me in a box. I am glad to report that I have totally changed my thinking about who I am and what I can do, which means that there is now a new truth that has set me free from what I previously considered to be truth. I am an author, I am creative, I am a source of joy and inspiration for many people, but there are times when I haven't walked in those truths. That's not true any longer.

How about you? Are there any truths about yourself that haven't set you free but tied you up? If so, then those things aren't the truth at all! Spend some time meditating on these ideas that have limited your ability to create, to be purposeful. Who knows, maybe you'll be up tomorrow night like I'm up tonight, allowing the truth to do its job, and that is to set you free.

Live to Live Again

I have come to the conclusion that you can actually live life at least twice, probably more. That's right, you can live two lives. I'm not talking about reincarnation or leading a double life, but rather experiencing your life events on at least two separate and distinct occasions. How is that possible? I'm glad you asked. To get the answer, you will have to read on.

LIVING LIFE *BEFORE* IT HAPPENS

I read something in a book by Matthew Fox's entitled, *Creativity*, and it got me thinking about living twice. Fox wrote:

> Anais Nin once said: "We write to taste life twice." I agree. I think we write to taste life twice, and we paint and dance and sing and compose and do all art to "taste life twice." This opportunity to taste life twice is an invitation to go deeper, to miss nothing, to tell others, to experience the joy a second time in the telling and in handing on the depth and mystery of life. When we behold, we become so struck by what it is we want to share. We call that sharing "art."[2]

That quote got me thinking about what Stephen Covey wrote in *The 7 Habits of Highly Effective People*. Covey said everything that is created is created twice: first in the mind or heart and then in reality. When you create a business, for example, you are living that business twice—

21

once in the theoretical and then the practical. Someone else suggested that our lives are being recorded and will be played back to us in eternity, where we will either weep with joy at the opportunities we took advantage of, or with grief when we see the opportunities we missed.

Since you will live your life twice, either in regret or joy, it is essential that you first focus your mind on what gives you joy and then make every effort to **do** it. I write *The Monday Memo* in my mind all week and then I sit down on Sunday to actually write it. I dreamed about starting my business and ministry and now I get to conduct business all over the world. In both cases, I enjoy my work **before** I ever do it. There's another way, however, that I can live twice, and you can join me and do the same. That's the way God made us to behave.

RELIVING LIFE *AFTER* IT HAPPENS

When I write, I get to enjoy life again **after** it happens. I have re-lived safaris, trips, successes, recoveries, book signings, and insight by recording what I felt, thought and did in written form. I have often told people that I write not only for others but also for myself. I often get more from my work than others ever could.

At times I have even relived my most painful memories by counseling and teaching people about what I learned from those experiences. They were difficult to live through once, but I have used those failures to make them (and me) into something that could help others. In some ways, I have relived those mistakes, made them right, gave them new meaning by distilling the most important lessons to be learned and then I have creatively shared them with my audiences.

Since you have many creative ideas, you want to act on those that will provide the greatest benefit for you and others as they are experienced over and over again. I have chosen writing and teaching as my main creative expressions.

My books will outlive me and my teaching can help shape lives and destinies. What can you do? Can you write poetry or screenplays, paint pictures or develop a cure for a problem that plagues mankind?

You can go through life experiencing things only once, reacting and allowing things to happen, or you can release your creativity and help make them happen or give them new meaning, thus living them at least twice. I hope you will choose the creative path that, even though more difficult, produces greater rewards and benefits for you and others. Have a great week!

Timing and Seasons

I hear people say they are concerned about timing or the right season to do this or that creative thing. They don't want to miss or get ahead of the Lord, so they watch and wait for God's timing. This is am important issue when it comes to acting on your creative ideas, so let's look at it more closely. When asked about timing, I usually give the same response; "Timing is pretty much *irrelevant!*" You will have to read on to see in what context I make this comment.

TIMING IS IRRELEVANT

Perhaps I should say that timing as a planning tool is overrated. I maintain it is *impossible* to know what time or season you are in until you are in it. Therefore why waste any time by trying to discover the right time, thus slowing down or casting doubt on what you were about to do? Let me explain it another way.

How do you know for sure that you have a good idea? Is it *before* or *after* you implement the idea? You may suspect it is a good idea *before*, but It is usually *after* you take steps to carry it out that you know for sure. If you are waiting for the right time to apply any good idea, you may never take action. That is why I say timing is overrated as a consideration when you look to step out and do something.

Perhaps two passages will strengthen my case. The first is found in Ecclesiastes 11:4-5:

> Whoever watches the wind will not plant; whoever looks at the clouds will not reap. As

you do not know the path of the wind, or how the body is formed in a mother's womb, so you cannot understand the work of God, the Maker of all things. Sow your seed in the morning, and at evening let not your hands be idle, for you do not know which will succeed, whether this or that, or whether both will do equally well.

The second is from the four lepers in 2 Kings:

Now there were four leprous men at the entrance of the gate; and they said to one another, "Why do we sit here until we die? "If we say, 'We will enter the city,' then the famine is in the city and we will die there; and if we sit here, we die also. Now therefore come, and let us go over to the camp of the Arameans. If they spare us, we will live; and if they kill us, we will but die" (2 Kings 7:3-4).

WHAT'S TIMING TO A LEPER?

The four lepers saw their condition as urgent. They were less concerned about looking bad or "missing God" than survival! It is **not** faith to want to know the timing and steps you must take to succeed. It is presumptuous! God does **not** owe you an explanation before you take the first steps in obedience. To think He does is to expect more than God gave Abraham. God told Abraham to set out. When Abraham wanted to know where he was going, the Lord basically responded, "I'll tell you when you get there."

If you don't identify with the lepers, you will then think you can "wait on the Lord." If you identify with their situation and see yourself in a need to act and have faith, then you will act **today** on your creativity, ideas, goals and dreams. Have you had enough of being where you are? Then step out and be less concerned about timing and more about finding fulfillment and creative expression.

Let me close with one more thought. I hear people say, "I don't want to get ahead of the Lord." I say, go ahead and try! If Ephesians 3:20-21 is true (and it is), there is **no way** you can get ahead of Him: "Now to him who is able to do immeasurably more than all we ask or imagine, according to his power that is at work within us, to him be glory in the church and in Christ Jesus throughout all generations, for ever and ever! Amen."

Dream big and then step out to see what happens. Be free to move out and about, knowing that you can't get ahead of God and you won't fully please Him **until** you act in faith, faith that the time is now to do the will of God.

Succccccess

I know I misspelled success, which only has two c's. At one point, I did a series on the "five c's of succccccess" and naturally spent five weeks unpacking that topic. If you think succccccess isn't a consideration for you, read these words from Psalm 1:1-3 in the Good News Translation and you may need to reconsider:

> "Happy are those who reject the advice of evil people, who do not follow the example of sinners or join those who have no use for God. Instead, they find joy in obeying the Law of the Lord, and they study it day and night. They are like trees that grow beside a stream, that bear fruit at the right time, and whose leaves do not dry up. **They succeed in everything they do**" (emphasis added).

With that in mind, let's look at the second c in succccccess, that being creativity.

YOU ARE TOO!

In 2006, I had a startling revelation and changed my purpose statement from "I *bring* order out of chaos" to "I *create* order out of chaos." It was then that I accepted the fact that I am a creative person, something I had denied up to that point. I began to write and teach about creativity after that, and I have many *Monday Memos* devoted to the subject of creativity.

Over the years, I have also collected creative life expressions from *Monday Memo* readers and posted that collection on my website. You can find that list in the Appendix of this book, or online, titled, "Samples of Creative Expressions." Once you read that list, I hope you will come to the same realization I did: You are a creative person, too!

CREATIVITY FOLLOWS CURIOSITY

The first c in succcccess is curiosity. Once you are curious and decide to follow your heart and what interests you, it is time to express your creativity. You can then begin to structure your world and invest your time in such a way that your creativity can take shape as a practical expression of who you are. I am interested in writing, and have been since I was young. So in 1995 at the age of 45, I started to pursue my interest and today I write every day to an audience all over the world.

As of this book, I have written 22 other books, 700 *Monday Memos*, finished a verse-by-verse devotional on the entire New Testament, and have written a daily devotional online featuring a question from the Bible every day for the last six years. This term I am teaching two classes and have a few other creative projects and ideas in the works.

I love to do media but got tired of waiting for people to invite me to be part of their media world. What did I do? I started my own online broadcast, *Ministry Beat*, which is live via the Internet every week. I launched a new show on AM radio and my online television show is up and running.

You don't have to do any of those things that I am doing to be creative. You just have to be yourself. You cannot be fighting yourself, however, and be creative. My experience is that most people (perhaps even you) are trying to talk themselves *out* of their creativity instead of into it. I hope you are encouraged to look at your creativity in new ways. You cannot be succcccessful without employing it, but you cannot employ it if you deny it even exists.

Creativity
Turned Tradition

If you have ever heard one of my purpose presentations, you probably heard me start at Acts 6:1-7, where the apostles chose men to carry out the work among the widows. The people elected these men to serve or minister to the widows in the church, and the Greek word for service here is *diakonia*, from which we derive our modern church office of or word *deacon*.

Many churches have taken this passage and turned it into a model for church government and service. In some churches, the deacons are the ultimate governing position; in others they are people who serve by doing practical things in the church like building care, women's ministry and the like. The goal here is not to debate which approach to deacons is correct. The goal is to show that any approach to deacons as a church institution misses the point altogether.

The original deacons were not about church government or tradition; they were simply a creative solution to a new problem.

THE BACKGROUND

As best I can tell, there was no biblical concept that the apostles followed to elect and commission the deacons in Acts 6. They simply followed this logical progression; 1) Jesus had instructed them to care for the poor; 2) most widows were poor in the early church if they had no other family to care for them; 3) as the church grew, the number of widows grew from those outside the ranks of the Hebrew residents in Jerusalem; 4) the apostles were being called upon to address this problem that had never before been faced; 5) they addressed this problem creatively and used wisdom to come up with a solution.

They were not instituting a church office in Acts 6, but rather an approach the church should be taking to address life's problems and challenges, whether in or outside the church. They were setting a precedent and not establishing a tradition.

THE IMPLICATIONS

When I think of creativity, I think of the verses you have already studied in Proverbs 8:22-31. Wisdom was there at God's side when He created the universe. As we discussed in essay three, wisdom is closely related to creativity, which leads to my definition of creativity: *the wise application of knowledge to existing problems or opportunities in such a way that something new emerges.*

In Acts 6, the problem was the widow care. The knowledge or biblical precedent that existed was Moses appointing helpers when he was overwhelmed; elections were also common in Israel to elect synagogue leaders. So the apostles applied existing knowledge in a new way - a wise way - to address a current problem and the result was creativity: a group of men who we call deacons today.

What is my point? The church should be the bastion and vanguard of creativity. We have the Creative Spirit of God in our midst. We should not be looking to solve new problems with the solutions of the past. We become bound to and trapped by our traditions when we don't see creativity as a function of the church and believers, or when fear causes us to retreat to the tried-and-true **procedures** rather than experiment with new **applications** of tried-and-true wisdom principles.

I urge you not to settle for what's been done, but

pioneer what's been done into what has never been done. The world is waiting for your poetry and your business ideas. When you do, you will be working with the wisdom of Proverbs 8 that was present when God created and structured the world. There is no greater creativity with which you and I can work.

Provision Anxiety

Anxiety is a form of fear, which we are going to discuss in Section Three. For now, I want to discuss a form of anxiety that will hinder your ability to create and that is anxiety about money. How often I have had a good idea only to dismiss it a few minutes later because of provision anxiety—where will I get the money to do that? That won't make me any money, will it? How will I feed my family? It's just an idea but I tend to immediately start thinking about cash and, when I do, the idea generally flies away as quickly as a bird that had come to nest only to find a "beware of the cat" sign.

I have reflected on the cloud that followed Israel in their wilderness wanderings. This cloud led them by day and became a pillar of fire by night. I had always thought this cloud was for guidance only. When it moved, Israel moved and when it stayed, so did Israel. That is part of what the cloud did. Yet I never thought that the cloud was also there for protection. There were millions of people and animals traveling in the scorching heat of the Middle Eastern desert, so the cloud had to protect them from all the elements.

What's more, God sent them manna to eat and water to drink in the desert. The Lord never had them learn how to exist in the desert by learning desert-survival tactics. They never made peace with their surroundings. He was able to provide for and protect them in the harshest of conditions and He did it for 40 years.

Now if God did that for Israel, what can He do for you and me? He certainly can't and won't do any less! Why worry about provision? God is capable of giving whatever you need and He knows what you need before you ask.

I am not saying that provision isn't important, for often when I tell people to focus on the idea and not the money, they think I am ignoring their money needs. I am not. I am not telling them to quite their jobs so they can create. It's just that I know that provision anxiety can stop anyone in his or her tracks, even a seasoned and creative faith warrior. You don't have to know who will publish your work or fund your business before you make plans to start and finish either. You just have to allow the creativity to flow, free from the effects of anxiety.

What could you dream today if provision anxiety didn't butt in? What plans could you make? What could you create or begin to create? I urge you to reflect more on God's ability to provide even in a desert and then apply what you learn to your own situation. Oops, gotta go. That idea bird that flew away earlier just came back and this time I want to welcome her along with the creative ideas she brings.

Your Role in Creativity

In Section One, we looked at some spiritual guidelines and principles where creativity is concerned. In this Section, we will look at your response to creativity, the role you play in making it happen. Too often people have pushed their creativity onto the Lord, crediting Him for all their work (the Lord gave me this idea) but blaming Him also when they produced nothing (the Lord hasn't released me to do this or that). It may be true that the Lord laid something on your heart or not, but in this section I want to make sure you are responding correctly and properly assigning credit and blame.

There are many hindrances to your creativity as you will read in this section and the next. Adam's creativity was given and directed by God, but Adam's sin resulted in fear, shame and embarrassment that caused him and Eve to hide behind fig leaves and a bush when God came calling. As we read in Section one, Adam had named the animals God brought to him. While the Fall did not eradicate Adam's creativity, it did taint it. It has been that way ever since.

Choose Wisely

It seems that man currently has three choices where creativity is concerned. In other words, you have three choices and I urge you to consider these options and then choose wisely. Here they are as I understand them:

OPTION 1: Refuse

1. **You can refuse to be creative**. That doesn't mean God doesn't love you; He does. That doesn't mean you are not saved. You are if you put your faith in Christ. You can, however, simply refuse to confront your fear and release your creativity. The interesting thing is you can't help but be creative, when you consider your ability to talk, reason, manage time, have children, start businesses, and the like.

Yet even while doing all that, you can refuse to use your creativity to express your purpose as Adam and Eve were commanded to do in the Garden: "God blessed them and said to them, 'Be fruitful and increase in number; fill the earth and subdue it. Rule over the fish in the sea and the birds in the sky and over every living creature that moves on the ground'" (Genesis 1:28). You can reject your mandate to be fruitful and rule, all the while maintaining a relationship with the Lord through prayer, reading and daily service.

OPTION 2: Rebel

2. **You can use your creativity for your own ends.** This is a subtle (or not-so-subtle) form of rebellion that tries to maintain control over creativity. Someone who doesn't know the Lord is generally in this condition, for they take

what God has placed in them but use it for selfish or self-willed purposes. Anyone who produces vulgar art, crude poetry or obscene films, just to name a few examples, is taking their God-given creativity and using it for ungodly means. Now a refusal to be creative as outlined in option one is a form of rebellion, but this second option actively seeks to use creativity for *anything* besides godly purposes.

A good example of this kind of creative rebellion is found in Genesis 10:8-10a: "Cush was the fatherof Nimrod, who became a mighty warrior on the earth. He was a mighty hunter before the Lord; that is why it is said, 'Like Nimrod, a mighty hunter before the Lord.' The first centers of his kingdom were Babylon . . ." Nimrod used his creativity to build his own kingdom and Babylon always represents an earthly kingdom that was established and existed to oppose God's rule and kingdom on earth.

OPTION 3: Reconcile

3. You can bring your creativity under the Lordship of Christ. Your third option is to surrender your will where you creativity is concerned to God's will and plan for your life. When you do this, you confront your fears, put aside your concern for what others think and do what is in your heart to do. When you do this, you accept the fact that Jesus came not just to reconcile your spiritual life to God, He came to reconcile all of you to God: " . . . and through him to **reconcile** to himself **all things**, whether things on earth or things in heaven, by making peace through his blood, shed on the cross" (Colossians 1:20 emphasis added).

Clearly then, options one and two are "sin," which is a word that simply means "missing the mark." When you avoid or trash your creative urges, you are missing the mark for your life, falling short of God's best for you. Generally, option one is where many Christians live. It is not an open or evil refusal, it is simply allowing fear to provide rational reasons why now is not the right time to write, travel, learn new languages, go back to school or sing. While those reasons may seem rock solid, they pale in the truth of what you know to be true: With God, all things are possible.

I trust you will shun option one, avoid two and wisely choose option three as the only viable place for a believer submitted to God's will to exist and thrive. When you choose wisely, you can be sure of God's help in your creative endeavors. Choose options one or two and you will create, but it will not be for the purpose God has chosen. As the title urges you, I pray you will choose wisely from the three options available to you.

Perfectionist Anxiety

Quiz question: How many ways are there
to receive change for one US dollar bill?

1) 47   2) 293   3) 63   4) 176   5) 117
(answer later)

Anxiety has a way of killing creativity. It's almost as if the best of your creative energy gets redirected to coming up with all kinds of reasons why what you want to create won't be any good, how no one will like it and reasons why you are not the person to make it happen. Some of my anxiety in creating is that I am a perfectionist. I want what I do to be good. No, I take that back. I want what I do to be great. No, that's not quite right either. I want what I do to be perfect! Yes, that's it. I just don't want the **right** way; I want the ***perfect*** way, the best way in the universe, the galaxy, in God's creation. I think you get the point.

I will wait to start something until I have a reasonable assurance that what I do will be perfect, or I will wait to start until I have a deadline to meet ("It wasn't my fault that it isn't perfect; I didn't have enough time."), or I won't ever start at all because I am not sure what the perfect creation would be or how to produce it.

Just this week I put off writing and doing simple things because I was afraid (no, not shaking in my shoes fear, but just fearful enough) what I would do or write would not be the best. I put something off until tomorrow just in case there was something I wasn't seeing that would prevent me from doing the perfect thing, whether it be an email, a phone call or writing the foreword to someone's book.

Often there is not just one road to a certain destination, there are a few. Now usually one route is the fastest route and that is one I should always take, correct? But what if there is a traffic jam on that "quickest" route? Then the next fastest route becomes the best route to take. But what if there are toll charges on that second fastest route and I don't have any money for the tolls? Then I can take the third route because it is still faster then the traffic-snarled first option and cheaper than the second option. But it's autumn and I want to see the pretty leaves changing colors on the way to my destination and that means I will take the fourth route, which is suddenly better than my other three options, even though it requires more time.

My point is that perfect is relative. Sometimes you produce what you can with the time you have and that has to be good enough. At times, you worked with what you knew at the time and, although less than perfect, you give yourself permission to do "good" work under the conditions.

The answer to the question at the top of the post is number two. There are 293 ways to make change for a dollar bill. What's the best way? It depends on what you need and the available change that someone has to give you in return for your dollar. I may need four quarters for parking, but someone may only have two quarters and five dimes. Since there's no one else around to give me change, I don't agonize. I say, "Give me the two you have. It's good enough for now."

So is anxiety over the best way to do something got you stuck? Then you have to talk yourself out of your dilemma by saying, "John, this isn't worth the time you are wasting on it. Get started and adjust along the way. You've done this before. You can do it again." Or "John, you know you are a perfectionist, so stop sweating the best way in the universe and get started on the best way you know of today."

Don't allow perfectionism to rob you and the world of the joys that your creativity can produce. Face your fears and your inordinate desire for the perfect whatever, and get started today. You'll be glad you did and your confidence will grow over time. By the way, anyone got change for a dollar?

Your Role in Creativity

Do you consider yourself a creative person? What creative outlets do you have, or rather how many do you give yourself permission to have? For most of my adult life, I did not give myself permission to pursue creativity and I wasn't open to the fact that I am creative. My self-image was that of an administrator and creativity and administration were at odds with one another—or so I thought.

Are you creative? If your answer is no, then perhaps you need to expand the way you view creativity and, consequently, view yourself. If you are open to that possibility, then I urge you to read on.

ADAM'S CREATIVITY

As I explained in Section One, Adam was made by God to be creative and we are Adam's children. After God created Adam, He invited Adam to express his creative process by naming the animals:

> "Now the Lord God had formed out of the ground all the beasts of the field and all the birds of the air. He brought them to the man to see what he would name them; and whatever the man called each living creature, that was its name. So the man gave names to all the livestock, the birds of the air and all the beasts of the field" (Genesis 2:19-20).

Adam decided what the animals were to be called; it was an expression of his creative dominion in the Garden.

Now this is *not* what happened. God brought an animal and Adam stared at it, dumbfounded. After an awkward silence, God leaned over and whispered in Adam's ear: "Zebra," and Adam said, "Zebra! God said, "Very good." Then God brought another animal and the same scenario repeated itself, with Adam simply giving back to God what he heard God say.

That is the image some believers have of creativity. God "lays it on their hearts" and they respond. What's wrong with this picture of creativity? It makes man simply a receiver, sort of like an antenna for heavenly broadcasts. I don't think when I make someone laugh that God put that humorous comment "on my heart." God gave me my humor gift and I use it creatively when I observe some situation, see the funny side to it and express it. That gift is mine to use – or misuse. God determined I would make people laugh, brings me the situations and then I creatively interpret them.

YOU ARE JUST LIKE ADAM

I hope you get the picture. Like Adam, you are creative and God wants and needs you to express your creativity in everyday life. Stop saying you aren't creative—you are! And stop seeing yourself as simply taking dictation for God's creative thoughts. That is part of your creativity, but it's not all of it. If you need help understanding just how creative you are, don't forget the list of creative expressions included in the Appendix and posted on my website. Take a look at that list and see how many expressions are present in your life and then, settle once and for all your perspective of your own creativity.

Then you will see yourself as creative, which is just how the Lord wants you to see yourself. Once you see yourself as creative, give yourself permission to pursue and release creativity in ways not possible up to this point in your life. As you do, you will have found your role in the creative process – to accept and express!

No More Excuses

I read something from Seth Godin almost every day and I have also read almost all his books. I have never met Seth (I hope to one day), but I feel like I know him. He was the one in 2001 who influenced me to start writing the *Monday Memo* after I read his book *Permission Marketing*. I try to pattern my writing on his. I admire the influence he has had in the business world and his relentless effort to produce relevant material that touches lives. Recently I received his daily blog and I include the content here for your reading enjoyment:

> Just ten years ago, what difference could you possibly be expected to make?
>
> How could you make music without getting picked by a record label, or help the local community garden more than showing up on Saturday to pull weeds? How could anyone expect you to change a conversation, or raise enough cash or move the needle more than a little?
>
> Today, armed with Mailchimp and Indiegogo and Vimeo and Meetup and a dozen other nearly free tools, you can make quite a ruckus.
>
> You can organize a hundred or a thousand people and get them in sync with a weekly newsletter. You can tailor goods or services or a cause to a small group of people that really want to hear

about it and really want to spread the word. You can self publish to your thousand true fans, you can host an event or a dozen events, you can enable your work to become famous to the crowd that matters.

Pick yourself. If you care enough.[3]

In other words, Seth is telling you and me, "No more excuses!" There is no reason why you are not publishing, recording or writing, except that you are afraid. You are taking the best of your creativity and weaving elaborate excuses in your mind that justify your inactivity. No more. What's more, don't try to touch everyone. In Seth's words, just find the "crowd that matters" to you.

I write and publish every day, sometimes twice a day, every day of the year. I determined in 2001 that there would be no more excuses and I have stayed true to my vow. As of this writing, I have produced 700 weekly *Monday Memos* and finished a verse-by-verse commentary on all 8,000 New Testament verses. I have written 22 books. I have five weekly radio shows and one weekly television show. That's what I have done. Now what can you do?

Thanks, Seth, for your relentless, ongoing encouragement. It may not have touched everybody, but it certainly touched me. I hope I can be counted among the crowd that matters to you.

Week #18

Ideas to Cash

I regularly meet with a group to talk about, encourage, showcase and study creativity. This group we call G1 (for Genesis 1:1, since we are doing the work of creativity the Creator assigned), has met since June 2013. Some people bring things to share and some just listen, but all speak of struggles, fears, and breakthroughs in creativity. The two hours we allot to meet always moves by quickly.

I had some insight into creativity from the story of Jacob in the Old Testament and thought I would include it in this book for your consideration. It's an unusual story, so I hope I am doing it justice as I apply it to your creative work.

"SPOTTY" PAYMENTS

When Jacob was preparing to leave his conniving father-in-law Laban, he proposed a plan that he would take all the spotted and speckled sheep as his payment for years of service. To Laban's surprise, Jacob proposed that all the existing spotted and speckled sheep be taken from the flock and only the yet-to-be-born spotted and speckled be Jacob's. What a strange plan, for how could Jacob expect to gain any not solid colored sheep if they were all removed before they could mate and reproduce? Laban was all too happy to comply and put a three-day's journey between his flocks and Jacob's so there would be no possibility, or so he thought, of Jacob getting any of his sheep.

Jacob had a divine plan, however, a flash of brilliance and creative insight that made him a wealthy man. We read in Genesis 30:37-43:

Then Jacob took fresh rods of poplar and almond and plane trees, and peeled white stripes in them, exposing the white which *was* in the rods. He set the rods which he had peeled in front of the flocks in the gutters, *even* in the watering troughs, where the flocks came to drink; and they mated when they came to drink. So the flocks mated by the rods, and the flocks brought forth striped, speckled, and spotted. Jacob separated the lambs, and made the flocks face toward the striped and all the black in the flock of Laban; and he put his own herds apart, and did not put them with Laban's flock. Moreover, whenever the stronger of the flock were mating, Jacob would place the rods in the sight of the flock in the gutters, so that they might mate by the rods; but when the flock was feeble, he did not put *them* in; so the feebler were Laban's and the stronger Jacob's. So the man became exceedingly prosperous, and had large flocks and female and male servants and camels and donkeys.

PRAY FOR MONEY

This strategy seems a bit weird, but it worked. Later when Jacob was talking to his wives who were Laban's daughters, he said this in Genesis 31:10-13:

> "And it came about at the time when the flock were mating that I lifted up my eyes and saw in a dream, and behold, the male goats which were mating *were* striped, speckled, and mottled. Then the angel of God said to me in the dream, 'Jacob,' and I said, 'Here I am.' He said, 'Lift up your eyes and see *that* all the male goats which are mating are striped, speckled, and mottled; for I have seen all that Laban has been doing to you. I am the God *of* Bethel, where you anointed a pillar, where

you made a vow to Me; now arise, leave this land, and return to the land of your birth.'"

I don't understand it all, but God gave Jacob a creative strategy and prospered him with an idea. Jacob had to follow through on the idea to get the financial blessing. I have discovered that sometimes you pray for money and God gives you an idea. You have to convert that idea into action and only then does the money come. There are no shortcuts and no winning the lottery. Jacob got the creative inspiration, had to implement what he saw and over time he became wealthy. I will end with this question: Do you have any creative ideas that you need to convert into action and then into cash and wealth?

One Word

A few years ago, my purpose statement changed. My purpose didn't change, but my statement did. People often ask, "Can your purpose change?" or "Can you have more than one purpose?" I always answer, "No," to both questions. Yet now I am saying my purpose definition or description did indeed change. Am I confused? Have I changed my mind? To find out the answers to those questions, you will have to read on.

ONLY ONE WORD

For many years, I stated that my purpose was "to *bring* [or make] order out of chaos." Then one day while driving in Zimbabwe, I saw that this definition wasn't correct. It wasn't so much that the definition was incorrect, but the way I interpreted my purpose was. On that fateful day in 2003, I realized that I don't *bring* order out of chaos, nor do I *make* order out of chaos. Rather I *create* order out of chaos. It dawned on me that I am a creative person and thus my statement should be [as has been since], "I create order out of chaos."

What a difference one word can make!

I had always viewed myself as an organized, administrative-type person. I saw musicians, songwriters, and poets as the creative people, while I existed to organize their creativity. Then one day I realized my ability to bring order *is* in and of itself is a creative act. I was defining my purpose by not including something I could not see. When I saw and gave myself permission to be creative, my life

49

changed and I started creating – or should I say continued creating, for I had in reality been creating for many years. That decision changed how I defined my purpose—and changed my life.

PERMISSION TO BE CREATIVE

A few weeks before I saw this change, I was heading to Uganda with a team from my home city. On the plane, the team leader asked me to fill out a form outlining my goals and objectives for the trip. Then she asked me to do something that would normally bring fear to my heart: She asked me to draw four pictures on the back of the paper to describe myself before, during and after the trip.

I actually felt my body stiffen as she asked me to draw those pictures, because "I can't draw," or so I thought. Right there on the plane I decided to face my fear of being ridiculed or of not being very good, and proceeded to draw four simple but effective pictures. They were the first four pictures I had drawn that I could remember since childhood.

After I drew those pictures, I took out a sheet of paper and listed all the areas in which I considered myself creative. Here is my list at the time: humor, consulting, conference and event coordination, *The Monday Memo*, the weekly Bible studies, my books, public speaking, my daily to-do list, my website and blog, the seminars that I teach and the two businesses that I started. These are all creative acts, so therefore I am creative! I **create** order out of chaos.

YOU TOO!

I write this to you because you are creative, too. The Creator made you in His image and part of that image is to create. You may not see yourself as creative, but you are. You may not have any original ideas (who does?), but you probably have ideas of how to creatively apply concepts that already exist in new ways.

Why not do what I did? Take out a piece of paper and write down all the ways that you are creative. Don't overlook activities like cooking, baking, gardening, floral design, letter writing, teaching, cleaning, repair work, interior design, and makeup and hair styling.

I also write this to help you overcome any bias that you may have against your creativity. Stop comparing yourself to others and don't compare what you create with what others create. This week let your creativity flow, just like I did with my four pictures I drew.

Facing the fact that you are creative may set you free to do things that have been in you to do all along. I have enjoyed my awareness of my creativity for many years now, and I believe the best is yet to come! Now I tell everyone and anyone that my purpose is to *create*, not bring, order out of chaos. What will you be able to do when you properly see yourself as creative and express it without a second thought? In all probability the world is in for a special treat as the creative you steps forth to sing the song that God put in your heart to sing.

It is Finished

I can remember in 2009 when I reached a goal I had set in 2001. I had worked toward that goal almost every day for more than eight years, and then it was finished. The feeling I had last was exhilarating, and I want you to experience something like it in your life over and over again. What was my goal? What took me almost every day for nine years to complete?

In 2009 I finished my last online Bible study, which meant I had completed a verse-by-verse commentary on the entire New Testament! (In case you were wondering, there are more than 7,000 verses in the New Testament and I wrote something for every one of them.)

Let's take a look at how it all came about.

EIGHT YEARS IN THE MAKING

After I completed a study of faith in 2001 (which later became *The Faith Files: Volume One*), I had an idea. I always said that "one day" I wanted to write Bible commentaries. I decided to start such a study, determining that I would look at four verses every day and write some devotional material for those verses. At the end of every week, I sent out those notes to those already receiving *The Faith Files*.

By studying and writing on four verses every day since 2001, I completed studies for all 27 New Testament books! Commenting on four verses a day every day enabled me to accomplish a huge task a little at a time. I exercised faith every day I sat down to write and I "saw" something in every verse along with ways to help the reader apply those verses to their daily walk. Needless to say, I have learned a lot since I began writing those studies and I hope my readers have, too.

IT IS FINISHED!

How did I know I was supposed to embark on this project? Was I certain that it was God's will? I can't say for sure, but I refer you to what Luke wrote in the opening of his gospel:

> Therefore, since I myself have carefully investigated everything from the beginning, **it seemed good also to me to write an orderly account for you**, most excellent Theophilus, so that you may know the certainty of the things you have been taught (Luke 1:3-4).

All I can say is that it seemed good to write and keep on writing. As people said they found the studies helpful, I just kept on going. The goal helped me reach the end. My creativity with God's help took care of the rest. I am glad to say that as far as my Bible studies are concerned, "It is finished!" (Although I am now editing them, republishing them online and looking to put them in published format for paper and ebook in the coming years.)

What about you? Do you have any "good ideas" like I had? What can you accomplish if you do just a little every day? I have found that most people won't be *anything* because they can't see how to do *everything*. They won't give a *little* because they can't give a *lot*. Won't devote a little time because they don't have huge chunks of time. I decided to do what I could do every day—four verses—and now I have completed my goal. There's no telling what you can do if you apply the same principle.

Stop procrastinating and take one step at a time. If you keep putting one foot in front of the other, who knows how far you can go. The Chinese say that the journey of a 1,000 miles starts with the first step. Why not take your first steps this week? Before you know it, you will feel what I felt when I finished this huge task that seemed so large at the start, but become much more doable when I broke it down into daily doses.

It is Finished, Too!

Not only did I finish my verse-by-verse Bible studies back in 2009, I also published my book, *The Revelation Project: A Fresh Look at the Last Book*. That book was part of the daily four-verse project that I described in the previous essay. My next goal of publishing my online Bible studies started with that book and I admit it is one of my favorite books I have written, mostly because I present a creative interpretation of one of the New Testament's most creative books, the book of Revelation.

How did I know I was supposed to publish this? How did I know it contained the best material? To find out how I answered those questions, you will have to read on.

A PHILOSOPHY FOR WINNING AT SOFTBALL . . . AND AT LIFE!

For eleven years, I lived in Alabama, a state in the deep South. Since I was home and travelling less, I played in a church softball league for nine of those years. Softball is similar to American baseball, but the ball is bigger and the pitcher throws it slower and underhanded. I was a better fielder than batter, and my teams won a more than they lost.

There was one team from another church, however, that was very good, and they beat us most of the time year after year. They didn't look as sharp as we did because we got new uniforms almost every year and they played in whatever they had. We practiced weekly yet we never, ever saw them on the practice field. They just knew how to win.

One night we met with some of their players to see if we could understand the secret of their success. We asked many questions, but then our coach asked their best batsman, "When you're at bat, do you have an offensive philosophy? Do you try to hit it over the fence or do you try to advance the runners one base at a time?" The man stared at our coach with a surprised look for a short minute and then answered, "We don't have any philosophy. We just hit it hard and wish it well."

That simple statement changed my life, and from that point forward became my philosophy not only for softball but also for life itself: Hit it hard and wish it well.

As I have sought to express my creativity, I have found this a great strategy to employ. Perhaps you too just need to stop thinking about what you want to do and just go "hit it hard and wish it well." In softball, sometimes you can do everything just right and not get to first base. Other times your technique may be all wrong, yet the ball off your bat lands in the right spot and you win the game for your team. Maybe you're waiting for perfection before you try something, or perhaps you're frustrated that you have done everything correctly as best you knew, but things haven't worked out so far. This week you need to overcome your hesitancy or discouragement and go to bat one more time.

"HIT IT HARD" IS IN THE BIBLE!

"Hit is hard and wish it well" is a principle found in the Bible. The writer of Ecclesiastes wrote thousands of years ago:

> "If clouds are full of water, they pour rain upon the earth. Whether a tree falls to the south or to the north, in the place where it falls, there will it lie. Whoever watches the wind will not plant; whoever looks at the clouds will not reap. As you do not know the path of the wind, or how

the body is formed in a mother's womb, so you cannot understand the work of God, the Maker of all things. Sow your seed in the morning, and at evening let not your hands be idle, for you do not know which will succeed, whether this or that, or whether both will do equally well" (Ecclesiastes 11:3-6).

Do you have any creative ideas on which you need to act? The time to analyze is over; the time to act has come. This week step to the plate and take your turn. Paint your picture, apply for the degree, start your business, or plan the vacation. Don't fret about uncertain results over which you have no control. Do what you can do and trust that it will work out for the good. Who knows, you may even hit a home run and win the game!

The Power of Curiosity

I touched on the topic of curiosity in Section One but we only started what I want to finish here. In this essay we want to look at a familiar story of Moses when he encountered the burning bush in the desert. You will see that a world-changing experience began with Moses following up on something that interested him, something that was out of the ordinary. As he went, God spoke and the rest as they say is history. Let's take a look now.

A BURNING BUSH

We know that Moses tended sheep in the wilderness for forty years! I have been to the Middle East numerous times and it is a hot place. Moses had to work in this heat year in and year out, and I am sure every now and then a dry bush would burst into flames due to the super-hot conditions. Then one day Moses saw something unusual that captured his attention:

> Now Moses was tending the flock of Jethro his father-in-law, the priest of Midian, and he led the flock to the far side of the wilderness and came to Horeb, the mountain of God. There the angel of the Lord appeared to him in flames of fire from within a bush. Moses saw that though the bush was on fire it did not burn up. So Moses thought, "I will go over and see this strange sight—why the bush does not burn up" (Exodus 3:1-3).

What was unusual about this bush is that it burned,

probably a common sight, but the bush was not consumed. It just kept on burning. Moses could have easily dismissed this sight and went about his business, but he decided to investigate further. Upon closer examination, he had a surprising thing happen: "When the Lord saw that he had gone over to look, God called to him from within the bush, "Moses! Moses!" And Moses said, "Here I am" (Exodus 3:4).

SO WHAT?

It is interesting that God did not call Moses and draw Moses to the bush. It was Moses' curiosity that caused him to pause and look, and then and only then did God call out to Moses and initiate a series of events that changed the course of history. In this order of events, first came Moses' curiosity, then his reaction, then God's call and finally Moses' response to God. What does this have to do with your creativity?

There are many people waiting for God's call. Perhaps you are one of them. Did you ever consider that the call may be in what interests you? You are busy and don't see how what interests you can add to your career, so you don't pursue what is in your heart. Because you don't trust what is in you, you go about your business and wonder why God is not answering your prayers to be used, promoted or creative.

Do you realize that it was Saul's interest, his obsession with persecuting Christians that led him to be a Christian and become the apostle Paul? If God can use Saul's misdirected interest to direct his steps, then God can use your curiosities to do the same. Creativity can start with investigating what piques your interest. Therefore I urge you to do something to satisfy your curiosity this week and see where it leads you. As you do, be listening for the voice of God and then follow His directions, just like Moses and Saul did. You may be surprised that the key to your creativity was hiding in your curiosity all along.

Down but Not Out

I love London. One year while I was there I went to see Handel's *Messiah* at the Royal Albert Music Hall. What a wonderful way to enjoy a timeless masterpiece of music and Scripture in the city where it was composed. That visit sparked one of my Christmas favorites from the *Monday Memo* archives, which I present to in this Section.

MESSIAH

The *Messiah* is considered by many to be the greatest musical feat in the history of mankind. Commissioned by a charity to produce a benefit concert, Handel wrote the *Messiah* in only 24 days. A musician once told me that someone trying to copy the Messiah could hardly do so in 24 days— that is the level of inspiration in which Handel operated when he wrote. Handel never left his house for those three weeks. His food trays remained untouched outside his office door. A friend who visited him as he composed found him sobbing with intense emotions. Later, as Handel groped for words to describe what he had experienced, he quoted St. Paul, saying "whether I was in the body or out of my body when I wrote it I know not."

What's even more impressive is that Handel wrote Messiah under extreme duress. The Church of England strongly criticized and opposed Handel and his previous Scriptural works put to music. At the age of 56, he had no money, often going out only at night so as to avoid his creditors. Handel performed what he considered his farewell concert and went home, fully expecting to end up in debtor's prison. Yet the first performance of Messiah in Ireland raised almost 400 British pounds for charity and freed 142 other men from debtor's prison in 1742. Of course the rest is history as countless millions have enjoyed and marveled at this work for more than 250 years. Handel also went on from there to enjoy tremendous success and popularity in his latter years.

So what does this have to do with you? Perhaps you are a person of purpose but feel frustrated, even defeated in your PurposeQuest. Maybe you find yourself down and out, discouraged and criticized, forgotten and a failure. Perhaps your finances are in poor shape. If that description fits you, read on, for I believe this Memo can restore your hope and faith. If that's not you, read on anyway, for you will probably enter that phase one day as you pursue your purpose.

WHAT TO DO WHEN
YOU ARE DOWN AND OUT

What should you do if you are in a season of "un-use," disfavor or inaction? I urge you to do three things if you are discouraged, disillusioned or dismayed. And if you're not, I urge you to find someone who is—you shouldn't have to look too hard—and encourage them in their dark time.

1. **Renew your faith in God.** Your success and purpose expression doesn't depend on your faithfulness; it depends on God's. Remind yourself that God can do anything, and then rest in Him. Handel went home to retire and perhaps thought it was all over for him. Yet God helped him, and a group found and commissioned him. God can and do the same for you.

2. **Keep preparing for your day of success.** I don't think Handel went home to retire and

abandoned music. Don't you abandon your love either. Keep writing, reading, learning and practicing. When the phone rings or the mail comes with your opportunity, you will be fresh and prepared, having worked in faith for the day of success.

3. **Be generous.** Handel wrote the *Messiah* for charity, even though he was destitute. What can you do for someone else, even though you are down and out? It is a good thing to do the unexpected in hard times, and giving something away definitely fits the bill when you are in need yourself. What better way to express your trust in God?

I'm grateful for God's help in my creative work and I hope you can find reasons to be thankful as well. If not, then just thank God for His faithfulness. At least you're still alive! Then take this *essay* to heart or share it with someone who needs it. I pray that as you do what I recommended above, you will see a creative breakthrough soon. When you're down and out, there's only one way to go and that's up. I pray that "up" times will find you soon and that you will do something to help that breakthrough come your way.

Books

In 2014 I went on a writing and publishing binge. Usually I try to publish one book every year. Last year I published three books and continued to write a fourth throughout the year. Here are some of my thoughts about the writing or creative process and I step back and consider what I have done and am doing:

1. Many people don't write because they say they don't have time. You have all the time in the world - 24 hours a day - so it's what you do with that time that determines whether or not you write and create.

2. Many times the "I don't have time" is just an excuse to cover fear and doubt.

3. Someone once said, "If you don't write when you don't have time, you won't write when you do have time." If you cannot write every day, can you set aside time one or two days every week and stick to your schedule?

4. It has been said that you don't produce a book, that a book produces you. I have found there is some truth to that. A book reveals your level of diligence, ability to keep and meet deadlines, and causes you to struggle to put things into words so that others will understand what you know and see.

5. You may not write because you don't know who will publish it. If you don't produce it, no one will publish it for sure.

6. You may not write because you don't know who will purchase it. If you don't write it, **no one** will buy it.

7. Where creativity is concerned, Franklin Roosevelt was correct: You have nothing to fear but fear itself! Fear is the great persuader, telling you all the reasons why you can't be the one to produce and publish. Don't listen to it.

8. The idea that six to ten weeks of uninterrupted time is needed to write is not realistic. You cannot stop your life to write, unless you are prepared to write full-time. Otherwise, you have to learn to write with the time you have available every day.

9. If you write two pages a day, in four months (with a few days off) you will have about 150 pages.

10. You may not write because you can't spell or don't trust your grammar. Hire an editor to correct that for you, but no one can write what's in your heart to say.

11. If you want to write interesting things, you must do interesting things.

What is your excuse? Why don't you write, sculpt, paint, rhyme or do what's in your heart to do? You will never create until you face your fears and doubts, and I have had to face every one of them listed above. I hope you will follow my example and face them but don't let them stop you. Press through and produce what you are capable of creating. In time, your doubts will diminish, especially when you have fruit to show for your efforts.

Hard Work

Let's review some of the points I have made about creativity up to this point in time:

1. **You are a creative person.** Whether you think you are or not, you were created by a creative God, the Creator, to be creative. Creativity is built into the essence of your being.

2. **Your creativity has enemies.** We saw how fear, perfectionism and comparison are the main hindrances to your creative expressions.

3. **There are many expressions of creativity.** We began to build a list of creative expressions, which included raising children, how you dress, repairs, gardening, time management and problem solving. A list of other possible expressions can be found in the Appendix and on www.purposequest.com.

4. **Jesus was a creative person.** Jesus was a carpenter, so He knew how to work with His hands. Then He used parables to creatively express the truths He came to proclaim. Since Jesus was and is creative, He can help you express yours.

CREATIVITY IS WORK

Now let's add one more point to the list: *creativity is*

hard work. Thomas Edison, the famous inventor and creator, once said, "Genius is 99% perspiration and 1% inspiration." This is an important point because many people are sitting around, waiting for a lightning bolt of inspiration to hit them before they begin to express their creativity. Since that lightning bolt seldom comes, they don't create, or at least don't think that what they want to do qualifies as creativity.

I was reading the creation story in Genesis and came across this verse: "By the seventh day God had finished the work he had been doing; so on the seventh day he rested from all his work" (Genesis 2:2). Why did God have to rest? He had to rest following His six-day *work* of creation. People ask me all the time, "How do you write your books?" My answer is always the same: "One page at a time, one day at a time."

I begin every day by sitting down at my computer to write my daily devotional that I send out to more than 1,000 people all over the world. I sit down Sunday night to write *The Monday Memo* and have done so since 2001. I do all this whether or not I feel creative or have any ideas. I begin to write and somehow my creativity flows. It doesn't just fall down from heaven, however, for I must work at it—*work* at being creative.

UNINSPIRED OR LAZY?

Could it be that we aren't more creative because we're lazy? All right, I'll be more specific. Are *you* not as creative as you could be because you are lazy? Is your lack of creativity due to a lack of discipline that doesn't allow you to sit down and write, or go to your workshop or pick up your paintbrush? Are you waiting for *inspiration* when you should be producing *perspiration*?

I was also thinking about the word *recreation* this week. Look at that word: re-creation. When you work at creativity, you need rest and re-creation. Why? So you can resume your creative expressions. If God rested from His creative work, then you and I will need to do the same. We recreate not just to have fun, however, but also to replenish what is lost in the creation process so we can start all over again. Recreation isn't a right; it's something you earn as you create. Recreation that is separated from the work of creation is selfish idleness and can be an idle waste of time.

What are you prepared to do this week with your creativity? I hope you have decided to work at it. Stop putting off until tomorrow the work that must be done today. As you do, plan for some rest and recreation. I trust that you will earn the right and create the need for some re-creation as you work to express your God-given creativity.

Mess Yourself Up

Do you know who makes sure I write my books? Do you know who requires that I write for four blogs, produce magazine articles, or develop my daily devotionals?

The answer: No one!

Now you may say, "Well, what about the Lord?" Yes, God has put those ideas and concepts in my heart and He positions me to do those things. Yet there is no one who can force me to write. I must do it on my own. It all starts with embracing the fact that I am a writer.

For many years, I never knew how to fill out my entry form as I went into foreign lands. The form would invariably ask for "Occupation" and I would put down administrator, pastor, consultant or teacher. Then one day I put down "author" and something snapped into place. I am a writer! I had given myself permission to tell others and it was a major breakthrough. I had never been asked at any passport control about what I do when I put down the other occupations. The first time I put down "author," the agent in the UK looked up at me and asked, "What do you write?" It proves the power of drawing attention and resources to yourself when you are honest about who you are and aren't.

I am an author and authors write. I have a goal to produce at least one book every year for the rest of my life. I have decided I will write every day, for now content to help people have an encounter with God's word through my devotionals. I want to produce a Bible with commentary pertaining to purpose and I have goals for what I want to do regarding starting libraries in Africa.

I came across a prayer, attributed to Sir Francis Drake in 1577, that I use as a seminar facilitator and I thought I would share it with you today. It goes like this:

> Disturb us, Lord, when we are too well pleased with ourselves, when our dreams have come true because we have dreamed too little, when we arrive safely because we have sailed too close to the shore.

> Disturb us, Lord, when with the abundance of things we possess, we have lost our thirst for the waters of life; having fallen in love with life, we have ceased to dream of eternity; and in our efforts to build a new earth, we have allowed our vision of the new Heaven to dim.

> Disturb us, Lord, to dare more boldly, to venture on wider seas where storms will show your mastery; where losing sight of land, we shall find the stars. We ask you to push back the horizons of our hopes; and to push into the future in strength, courage, hope, and love.

Have you become too pleased with yourself? Have you dreamed too little? Sailed too close to the shore? Ceased to dream of great things? If so, stir yourself up! Don't put off on God what only you can do. And don't underestimate your ability to ignore the Lord if you are relying on Him to stir you. It's time to mess yourself up and then put yourself back together in a more productive way.

Pray this prayer with me and then get to work. There are lives to be changed and worlds to be explored. There is no telling what can be done by people like you who aren't afraid of failing and who know how to disturb their world so that they can do more, see more and go to more places than they ever thought possible.

Fear

Fear plays such an important negative role in creativity that I decided to devote an entire section to help you control and contain its effects. The truth is, however, that I am not sure you will ever totally eliminate fear from your world as you seek to create. It is part of our fallen state as human beings. If you remember in Genesis 3, you saw Adam and Eve hiding from God, cowering in a bush clad with hastily made loin clothes. You are their children and will shrink back in fear and shame and must take steps to break free of that condition, especially if you want to create.

I include this Section with some concern that you will focus on fear and get more fear. Yet my hope is that the truth will set you free and that facing your fears will help you get free from them. One of the things I recommend regularly is that we celebrate our failures and in this Section, you will find out what I recommend that and how to go about doing it.

It's That Time Again

I have written about failure in many *Monday Memos*, and even instituted a worldwide "Celebrate a Failure Week." Here is how and why I have felt the need to do so.

THE GROUND RULES

For several years now, I have recommended that you take every chance to reflect on and talk about failure, its role in your life and the lessons you have learned from past failures. Here are some ideas of how to celebrate:

1. If you are a pastor, you can talk about failure in your Sunday services or during your midweek gatherings. Someone wrote me once that there is no failure in the Bible. See if they're right. If not, then share what you find that can help people who have failed. You have plenty of them sitting right in front of you every Sunday.

2. If you are a business leader, why not talk about failure with the other leaders and staff. Do you have any failures to celebrate as a business or team? What did you learn from them? What is stopping you from creating new failures? What could you possibly achieve today if you weren't afraid of trying and failing?

3. You can celebrate as a family. You may want to study a biblical character who failed, like Samson, Moses, David or Peter. Maybe there

is some family story of failure that can be discussed and examined. Maybe you can focus on a historical figure like Abraham Lincoln, Nelson Mandela or Winston Churchill, who were great leaders who experienced great failures or setbacks at some point.

4. Classroom settings need not be left out of this celebration. If you teach, I would imagine that you can find enough teaching material to make up a classroom session or two. History and science are full of failures that eventually led to success, of failures that provide significant lessons for your students.

WHY?

Why the need for such a celebration? And is it truly possible to celebrate failure? Should it not be tolerated at worst and avoided at best? We should celebrate failure since it is an inevitable part of life. We avoid failure because we believe it is somehow a measure of inadequate spirituality, and in some ways it is, because you will never measure up to the ideal of perfection on this side of heaven or the Lord's return. If you are going to do anything for God, whether to fulfill your purpose or achieve your goals, you need to embrace the learning process only failure can provide.

Here is a quote from one of my favorite authors, Parker Palmer, and what he said about failure in his book, *The Active Life:*

> If I allow my life to be deformed by the fallen angel called "fear of failure," I will never be fully alive. I will withhold myself from actions that might fail, or ignore evidence of failure when it happens. But if I could ride that fear all the way down, I might break out of my self-imposed

isolation and become connected with many other lives, because failure and the fear of it are universal. I would learn that failure is a natural fact, a way of discerning what to try next. I would be empowered to take more risks, which means to embrace more life, and in the process I would become more connected with others. The monster called fear of failure (or ridicule, criticism, or foolishness, or any of the other fears that are easy to regard as mortal enemies) would become a demanding but empowering guide toward relatedness.

But on *this* side of such an experience, we may wonder why we should go anywhere near the monsters, let alone ride them all the way down. After all, they are monsters, and they do harbor powers of destruction as well as of creativity. Even if riding the monsters is the only way to reach safe ground, there is no guarantee that we will get there. People have fallen off before the end of the journey and have been stranded in some bad places. So why take the risk of riding the monsters in the first place?

[The reason is that] some monsters simply will not go away. They are too big to walk around, too powerful to overcome, too clever to outsmart. The only way to deal with them is to move toward them, with them, through them. We must learn to befriend some of these primitive powers that seem so much like enemies. In the process we will find them working for us, not against us, working for life, not death.[4]

Of what are you afraid? Is a past failure or the fear of a future one keeping you ineffective and paralyzed? Are you so afraid of missing God's will for your life that you *are* missing God's will for your life? This is why we need a Celebrate a Failure Week every now and then. It's not to glorify failure but to set the stage for success. That may not make sense at this point, but if you follow along for the next few weeks, I think you'll understand how it works.

Get ready for a big celebration, for I'm sure you all have some colossal failures to celebrate and some important lessons to review. We want to get failure working for us and not against us, so with that in mind, let the party begin.

The Halls of Failure

As we continue to look at fear and failure, I want to talk about the halls of failure, of which there are quite a few in my country. These are places where thousand of people come every year to honor those who failed regularly and with distinction in their illustrious careers.

Where are these halls of failure, you may ask? There is one in Canton, Ohio, another in Cooperstown, New York and another in Springfield, Massachusetts, just to name a few. If you follow such things, you know that these are the locations of the baseball, football and basketball halls of fame. Let's talk about why I call them halls of failure.

FAILURE IGNORED

Let's first look at baseball. The best batters in baseball failed at least 65 percent of the time when they came to bat. The best pitchers failed as many as 40 percent of the time when they pitched, not to mention how many "non-strikes" they threw. The best fielders failed only about 10 percent of the time, but some of the managers remembered in the hall of failure lost almost as many games as they won.

In football, the hall of failure quarterbacks missed 50 percent of their pass attempts. The best running backs fumbled numerous times and the best defenders missed many tackles. In basketball, some of those enshrined in the hall missed 40 percent of their free throws. Others turned the ball over (gave it to the other team) hundreds of times and lost games for their team when it counted most—at the very end when they were the last ones to touch the ball.

You know these halls where the greatest players are memorialized are not called halls of *failure* but instead halls of *fame*. They are places where thousands pay money to go and remember the greatest players, *regardless* of how many times they failed. In fact, people seldom remember how many times they failed. Their failures are ignored in the face of the successes they enjoyed.

FAILURE FORGOTTEN

What about the players memorialized in these halls of fame? What is their attitude toward failure? The statistics I quoted above are accurate; they did indeed encounter many failures in their careers. The key to great success for them was that failure did not define who they were or the legacy they left. Consider Michael Jordan, perhaps the most famous basketball player of the modern era and these facts about him in his own words: "I missed more than 9,000 shots in my career. I've lost almost 300 games. Twenty-six times I've been trusted to take the game-winning shot and missed. I've failed over and over again in my life. And that is why I succeed."

The great players learn to manage and even forget their failures. They use them as a means to improve. They study what they did wrong and what they would do again if faced with a similar situation. They failed so much that they learned how to succeed. More importantly, they did not allow failure to define them because they did not quit.

What's your story? How many times have you failed? Truth be told, you probably haven't failed enough to be successful. Have you allowed past failure to limit your attempts to succeed today? Have you allowed the voice of past failure to coach your play today? I'm not referring to your sports career, but attempts to write, act, lead or parent. If you don't learn to forget failure, no one else will ignore it. That's why we learn to celebrate failure, so we can laugh at it and move on to success, however you define success in life.

If nothing else, take a moment now and then to reflect on the truth found in Romans 8:28: "And we know that in all things God works for the good of those who love him, who have been called according to his purpose." Think about how God has worked something good in you from your failure and then go out and do something great that your failure taught you to do.

Is Failure Spiritual?

As a write, I got a few rejection notices from publishers after I submitted a manuscript. I always took that failure as positive, for then I knew for sure that the publisher wasn't someone with whom I was supposed to work. Yes, I have had plenty to celebrate during my own Celebrate a Failure Week.

THE QUESTION

This week, let's consider whether or not failure is spiritual and if spiritual people who are following the Lord should expect to fail and then celebrate about it. Let me start with a quote from Thomas Merton's in his book, *New Seeds of Contemplation.*

> Perhaps we still have a basically superstitious tendency to associate failure with dishonesty and guilt—failure being interpreted as "punishment." Even if a man starts out with good intentions, if he fails we tend to think he was somehow "at fault." If he was not guilty, he was least "wrong." And "being wrong" is something we have not yet learned to face with equanimity and understanding. We either condemn it with god-like disdain or forgive it with god-like condescension. We do not manage to accept it with human compassion, humility and identification.

> Thus we never see the one truth that would help us

begin to solve our ethical and political problems: that we are *all* more or less wrong, that we are *all* at fault, *all* limited and obstructed by our mixed motives, our self-deception, our greed, our self-righteousness and our tendency to aggressivity and hypocrisy.[5]

Merton was saying that failure to face your own humanity causes you *not* to accept the humanity of others. Failure is part of being human. You cannot serve God in the hopes that He will save you from our propensity to fail. If God was willing to do that, for example, He would not have commanded you to forgive other people. He knew you would fail others and provided the means by which you could deal with it appropriately. God didn't say, "Now that you are mine, you won't be needing to forgive one another any longer." He was saying, "Come to terms with your failure toward one another by forgiving one another."

Those who take refuge in a false sense of spirituality as they try to avoid human failure have already failed. If you don't fail, you're not trying and if you don't try, you won't ever know which thing you **could** have done was the thing you **should** have done. If you don't fail, you deprive yourself of the great learning experience that learning can provide. If you don't fail, you won't fully know or understand God's love that is with you no matter what.

THE ANSWER

So is failure spiritual? Indeed it is, for it contributes to your spiritual growth by grounding you in your humanity. It's then that you know God's love and grace, and are able to share the same with your fellow failing humans, not from a position of superiority, but from a position of identity.

I pray you will have a profitable time reflecting on the role failure plays in the life of a spiritual person like you. I already have enough failures to cover the next ten

Celebrate a Failure weeks, and I'm sure I will collect even more material in the days ahead! With that in mind, I look forward to celebrating my humanity **and** my spirituality with you in an upcoming Failure Celebration. Thank God He still loves and uses you and me, even in the midsst of our human condition.

Is Failure Biblical?

I experienced some failures leading up to one of the Celebrate a Failure Weeks. All in one week, I had a bid for some training, which I thought was a pretty sure thing, postponed and I had a grant proposal turned down. I failed to get all the writing done I had planned and some physical challenges limited my effectiveness during a trip to Nigeria. All in all, it was a very good week! How many failures have you had lately? Probably not near enough for you to be a success.

In the last essay I answered the question of whether or not failure is spiritual. I came to the conclusion that it is. In this essay, I ask whether or not failure is biblical. For the answer to that question, you must read on -- but I think you have a hint as to what the answer is. Let's take a look.

BIBLE FAILURES

I can think of a number of prominent failures in the Bible. Here are some and you may think of more:

1. Abraham's decision to have a son through Hagar (see Genesis 16).

2. Moses' failure to circumcise his son, which almost cost him his life (see Exodus 4:24-26).

3. David's attempt to move the ark without following the directions for doing so (see 1 Chronicles 13).

4. Peter attempting to walk on the water and sinking (see Matthew 14:29-31).

5. Peter's denying he knew Jesus (see Mark 14:71-72).

6. Paul's sermon in Athens, which was technically brilliant but lacked results (see Acts 17).

7. Peter's hypocrisy in turning away from the Gentiles when the Jews arrived (see Galatians 2:12-14).

Obviously there are a lot of accounts of failure in the Bible because the Bible has a lot of stories about people, and people and failure go hand in hand. Someone once said that the Bible is not a collection of stories about good people seeking God, but of a good God seeking messed up people. Yet perhaps the most powerful failure story of all is the one that involved David and Bathsheba.

THE SECOND SON

I assume you are familiar with this story. If not, you can read about it in 2 Samuel 11 and 12. Bathsheba became pregnant by David while she was still Uriah's wife, so David had Uriah killed in battle. When all this came to light, the Lord took the life of David and Bathsheba's baby boy. What a failure! What a disgrace for the king and his legacy!

Yet David had taken Bathsheba as his wife and she got pregnant again. Now surely this child would also be under God's judgment. Surely the fate of this child would be like that of the first one. At least, that's what human wisdom would dictate. That, however, is not what happened: "She gave birth to a son, and they named him Solomon. The Lord loved him; and because the Lord loved him, he sent word through Nathan the prophet to name him Jedidiah [which means loved of the Lord] (2 Samuel 12:24-25).

Does this mean that the Lord condoned what David did? Absolutely not! Does this mean that you can go ahead and fail, assured that the Lord will eventually work everything out? Absolutely not! What does it mean then?

It means that God can bring something good out of any situation in which we have faith. David reacted so honorably when he was confronted with his sin, acted so nobly when the first baby died, that God had mercy. That's the point of celebrating failure. God is merciful! Failure is never the end, but often the means to a new beginning, one that is more glorious than anyone could have hoped. In our eyes, failure is terminal. From God's perspective, it's a chance to learn more about yourself and about Him. Only God could allow one of the world's wisest rulers to come from a union so marred by failure and sin.

Is failure biblical? What do you think? I don't know if it's biblical, but it sure is in the Bible. And if it's there, I know it will be present and relevant in the here and now. Therefore plan the party! Get the decorations ready. Armed with confidence that God has been and is with you, celebrating failure will prepare you to attempt new ventures and learn new lessons that will equip you for the ultimate success that God wants you to enjoy.

Is Failure Practical?

I trust you get the idea that I'm trying to instill in every reader the notion that there's no perfection this side of heaven, and that failure is a necessary albeit sometimes painful part of success, purpose and productivity. Let me continue to make my case.

LET'S CHANGE THE NAME

I've had many people tell me, "Dr. Stanko, I just can't celebrate my failures. They are still too painful, and they don't glorify God!" Even though I've written about this principle and even shared some of my own failures, you still may struggle with this concept of celebrating failure, too. That is why I'm proposing another name for failure, a name that is hopefully easier to accept. If you can't embrace "Celebrate a Failure" Week, how about "Celebrate Some Feedback" Week? It isn't as catchy, but I believe it's just as accurate.

You see, failure is simply feedback. The feedback tells you that you need to make an adjustment because you are off course. If you accept this feedback, then you can make the necessary changes that will put you back on track and help you succeed. The astronauts who went to moon had to make a course correction regularly. If they had rejected the feedback of where they were, they would and could have shot right past the moon. They accepted where they were, however, and then did what they had to do to make a course correction.

I believe that your pursuit of creative expression is similar to what those astronauts encountered. For example, you send your manuscript to a publisher and they reject it. You should simply see this as feedback. You can change your manuscript to make it more acceptable, try another publisher or write a whole new manuscript. If you experienced a broken relationship, you can reflect on that feedback and set a course that will make your next relationship more lasting and meaningful. If you started a business and you ran out of money, you can start again more intelligently as you use the feedback from the first business.

Failure is what you make of it. It can be devastating if you accept it as such. If you receive it as feedback, however, you can use it to do a better job and plot a new or revised course forward. The choice is yours.

WHO'S YOUR COACH?

I was watching a clip of American baseball spring training from Florida a few weeks. This clip showed a well-known batsman taking practice swings in the batting cage. Right behind the batter was his hitting coach, watching his every swing and giving him feedback. He was getting feedback on every swing, using that feedback to improve. When the season starts, that batter's batting average will be posted every day for all the world to see. He will have to face that feedback and then meet with his coach almost every day to stay on course and be all that he can be.

Baseball players aren't alone. Opera singers take lessons, and so do successful actors. Tennis players almost always have a coach who travels with them, helps them devise strategy, and provides immediate feedback on their performance. The most successful performers actually invite feedback—they encourage and even pay people to tell them where they are failing so they can improve. What about you? Who is your coach? What are you doing to encourage and process feedback?

I can answer the question in the title of this

week's post by saying, "Yes, failure plays a practical role in life and creativity." It helps you be the best you that you can be. If you are serious about being a creative person, you must learn how to handle feedback, even the painful kind. If something isn't working, you need to know that and learn what you can do to make it better.

Why is this so difficult for spiritual people to grasp? Why do we feel we have to do it alone? Why are we afraid to fail and learn from the failure? I leave you to come up with the answers to those questions in an upcoming celebration. When you celebrate the role of failure in your life, you need to assess how much feedback you are prepared to handle. That will determine what success level you will achieve.

Week #32

A Personal Failure

In 1993, I went to work for Integrity Music as the executive director of their ministry division called Worship International. It was and still is my favorite all-time job. I had the privilege of organizing worship conferences and events all over the world featuring worship leaders like Don Moen, Ron Kenoly, Marty Nystrom and Kent Henry. I attended almost every event as the organizer and director, and it was at those events that I started teaching on finding your purpose.

I loved the people I worked with, I loved the company and told God regularly that I could hold that position for the rest of my life—and I meant it! Then in 1995, we started losing money on the events we held. Do you know what my strategy was to turn things around? I decided to plan more events! we were losing money on our events, so I decided to do more of what we were losing money doing. Looking back, I can't imagine a worse strategy to adopt.

The results were predictable. In six months, we were out of business and I was out of a job! I was devastated! I had an offer to move back to Pittsburgh, the last place I wanted to be at the time, to work in a local church, a job I said I would not do again. Before we knew it, however, we were back where we didn't want to be doing a job we didn't want to do. Now that's how I define a colossal failure!

HOW CAN I CELEBRATE?

I received many comments over the years from readers describing terrible failures—broken relationships, bankrupt businesses and ministry disappointments. The common question from many was, "How can I celebrate such a terrible thing?"

You will celebrate your failure the way I celebrated the one I described above. I started out thanking God *in faith* for the pain and embarrassment. It is hard to rejoice at the time of the failure and even in the days and years that follow. When they happened I thanked Him in faith and pain; today I do it with joy and laughter.

I would not be the man doing what I am doing today if it wasn't for those failures. I learned so much and, to be truthful, I would do those things again, knowing what I knew at the time. I did the best I could, but things didn't work out. It was painful, but I lived and learned. Those failures didn't define me because I didn't allow them to define me. I only allowed them to teach me.

As you know by now, failure is important for your creative development. I teach and make money today telling people about my failures of yesterday. I apply what I learned from my failures to have unexpected success today. I didn't let failure stop me, and I encourage you not to let it stop you either. Failure is only the end if you allow it to be. Therefore, don't allow it, but rather define it as a tutor on the way to graduate school. When you get to the end, you will find that a few F grades led you to straight A's!

I Was Wrong

When I teach about leadership and creativity, of course I talk about failure. Perhaps you have heard me present or read my four-question series designed to help people understand the importance of failure:

1. Is failure a learning experience?

2. Do you learn more from failure than success?

3. Are you always to be learning and growing?

4. Should you fail as often as possible?

Usually, people answer "yes" to the first three questions, but answer "no" or not at all on question four. I have come to see that I have been misleading people on that fourth question and I am here this week to tell you that I was *wrong*, or at least incomplete in my thinking where question four is concerned. You will have to read on to understand where I was wrong.

AN IMPORTANT ADJUSTMENT

I was teaching a class recently and we were discussing failure. It was then I realized question four was incomplete. It should read:

4. Then hould you fail *on purpose* as often as you can?

Think of the most famous example of failure in the world of business: Thomas Edison's discovery of the light bulb. Edison experimented and failed with thousands of materials to find the correct filament that would burn and give light for a long period of time. While you can say that Edison failed thousands of times, he failed with purpose. He was trying to achieve something and the achievement was so important and valuable to him that he persevered and eventually found success.

If you just set out to fail so you can learn, your failure will not be tied to anything important and will not help lead you to any success. Therefore I was wrong when I urged you to fail. I am confident I am correct when I direct you to fail on purpose.

MORE EXAMPLES

A baby gets up every time he or she falls because the baby has purpose: learning to walk. You failed in school and gave wrong answer in the pursuit of learning. You did not hit every ball you swung at, did not make every goal you kicked a ball to score, and did not make every jump or foul shot you attempted. Yet you kept swinging, kicking and shooting because you had a purpose to win and improve. You could tolerate failure because you had purpose.

What are the implications for your creativity? It has important implications, for you will not tolerate or even allow failure unless it is in the pursuit of something that has overriding value, enough to keep you on the path to success no matter what the cost. What's more, you won't endure failure in searching for your purpose unless you see the value in the search and ultimate conclusion. Without that, you will be content with the status quo and endure failure because it helps you get what you want, which is to preserve the status quo.

I am excited about my newfound discovery and adjustment. What's more, it makes a lot more sense. You should not go out and fail just because it may help you learn, but you should be eager to fail if you are doing what is most important to you where creativity is concerned. You should be eager to write some bad poems on your way to writing good ones. You can mess up some paintings as you perfect your style and subject matter. You get the idea – failure is an important learning experience but only in regards to your creative purpose. Apart from that, failure is just what you have considered it to be – humbling and unpleasant. As a tutor, however, failure can still be one of the best teachers you have where success is concerned.

Failure P.S.

A few years ago my wife and I celebrated failure by moving into a brand new house! It's a lovely home and we are thrilled to still be living there. It has everything we want and need, in a part of town we like, overlooking a valley with lots of trees and hills. It has a full basement, from which we will run our PurposeQuest business. It's new construction and everything is, well, it's so new. What a blessing that home has already been.

What the home represents makes it all the more special, for it truly signifies a journey that included failures and heartache. Those failures only served to enhance our appreciation this week as we moved. When we moved out of our last house, it felt like the Bataan Death March. Psalm 126 best describes the journey into our new home:

> When the Lord brought back the captives to Zion, we were like men who dreamed. Our mouths were filled with laughter, our tongues with songs of joy. Then it was said among the nations, "The Lord has done great things for them." The Lord has done great things for us, and we are filled with joy. Restore our fortunes, O Lord, like streams in the Negev. Those who sow in tears will reap with songs of joy. He who goes out weeping, carrying seed to sow, will return with songs of joy, carrying sheaves with him.

THE JOURNEY

When I started PurposeQuest in 2001, it represented a failure of sorts. I had failed to start it earlier in life and had lost many opportunities. I was afraid, however, and put it off too long. When I left my church work to start the business, the people I had been with for many years were not happy and did not bless my departure. I found myself with no money, four books I had written, a purpose message and no place to go at 50 years of age.

Starting over proved to be a struggle. Before long, we found ourselves in debt, and I was traveling long distances to pursue business opportunities, often staying away from home longer than I wanted to stay. God was always faithful and we never lacked, but the pressure finally got to us in 2005. We decided to do what we had to do to downsize, pay off our debts and save some money to buy another home. I wish I could tell you that all my business decisions since 2001 have been good ones, but they have not. Yet I learned along the way and also found and sharpened my "voice"—my message and how to deliver it.

From time to time I listen to Barry Manilow's song, *I Made It Through the Rain*. I won't include the lyrics, but you can watch and listen to that song online along with a moving purpose tribute from Barry to his grandfather. Perhaps then you will understand some of what I felt when we got into our home and maybe it will encourage you along the way.

If that doesn't do it for you as we put the topic of failure to bed, then I know this last passage will. It's found in the short letter of Jude, verses 24 and 25, right before the book of Revelation. The verses are actually a prayer, and I hope you can hear me praying this for you as I edit this essay as a Failure P.S.:

> To him who is able to keep you from falling and to present you before his glorious presence without

fault and with great joy—to the only God our Savior be glory, majesty, power and authority, through Jesus Christ our Lord, before all ages, now and forevermore! Amen.

Amen and amen. Now go and do something great for Him!

Anxiety

I have been doing a lot of study and reflection on anxiety and the role it plays in procrastination. I was recently reading a book my sister-in-law recommended entitled *The Van Gogh Blues: The Creative Person's Path Through Depression*. Author Eric Maisel had this to say about anxiety:

> When we perceive a threat, we get queasy, light headed, confused, agitated, fatigued, nervous. We call these various reactions to a perceived threat by one name: anxiety. Existence threatens us in a thousand ways and therefore, anxiety is our constant companion. . . . Writing a short story, say, is really only a small threat to our self-esteem since if we do a poor job, we can revise our story or write a better one. But nature has decided that even these tiny threats must be taken seriously. As soon as we say, "I want to write a short story," waves of anxiety arise to keep us out of harm's way.
>
> The net result is that we do not write the story and do not make any meaning. Since we are not making meaning, depression strikes. The relationship between anxiety and depression, therefore, is direct and significant. If existence merely troubled us but didn't rouse so much anxiety in us, if we could hold our painting or composing as hard but not threatening, we would have a far better chance of making meaning and avoiding depression. If we heard ourselves say, "I

don't want to paint because I don't find painting meaningful," we could reply instantly, "The heck with you, insidious thought! I'm off to the studio!" But because the thought is threatening and because Nature hates threats, we are bathed in anxiety and stopped in our tracks. . . .

If you don't write your nonfiction book, which you have every reason to write and which you have been talking about for years, it is unlikely you will call your blockage a phobia and point to anxiety as the culprit. . . . Many of my clients I see complain of procrastination. Instead of starting off a Sunday turning right into their creative efforts, first they write in their journal, then they read the newspaper, then they have a third cup of coffee, then they head out to the laundromat. It turns out that they will do almost anything to ward off the anxiety they might feel if they said to themselves, "Time to create!"

While at work, they tell themselves that they will get to their novel or their symphony as soon as they get home, or after dinner at the latest. When they get home, they look at the ads that came in that day's mail, make dinner, do the dishes, and watch television until bedtime. Anxiety steals away their evening.[6]

Does that sound familiar? Since I identified anxiety as one of my main creative culprits, I have found it easier to write my school papers, do the research for my dissertation and complete other creative tasks. I am able to control my self-talk and say, "This is easy for me. I can do this in no time at all. It doesn't have to be perfect, but it will be the best I can produce!"

What about you? What role is anxiety playing in your lack of productivity and creativity? What are you prepared to do about it? More on anxiety later. You have enough to think about based on what I wrote above.

More on Anxiety

If anyone, including a Christian, is going to creatively produce, he or she must deal with the issue of anxiety, a topic which we began to address in the last essay. I am learning to deal with anxiety that keeps me from expressing my creativity and I see it all the time in many people whom I coach. Church people have a new repertoire of excuses that others can't use, excuses like, "I'm praying about it," "God hasn't released me to do that," "It's not God's timing," or "I don't want to get ahead of the Lord." Sometimes these expressions may be based in fact, but others times they are a mask for anxiety and fear.

In the previous essay, I quoted from Eric Maisel's book, *The Van Gogh Blues: The Creative Person's Path through Depression.* Let's continue with the excerpt that I began in that last essay:

> When a creator does this frequently enough and lets his [or her] anxiety about creating stop him [or her] from creating, he [or she] begins to feel like a weak, indecisive person. It is a very short step to even darker feelings of worthlessness and hopelessness. The end result of not knowing that he must brave his anxiety is that he ends up completely down on himself. Anxiety bests him and, to make matters worse, he then has to deal with the negative labels he pins on himself. This classic vicious cycle, where anxiety leads to a battered self-image and a battered self-image makes it harder to brave anxiety, defeats many creators.

Anxiety can debilitate any creator, even the most strong-willed and self-directing. A fiercely independent-minded sculptor may mention with a laugh that some friends visited his studio and hated his new work. On the surface, it looks like he's shrugged their comments off. Three weeks later, he complains of serious blockage. Doubts about his talent now make him anxious, his anxiety causes him not to sculpt, but the "why" of this is completely unknown to him. Anxiety has chalked up another victim.[7]

Has anxiety claimed you as a victim? I don't restrict the effects of anxiety to just the creative arts like writing or painting. It can hinder your ability to start a business, take a missions trip, teach a class, or go back to school. You can be so uptight about doing something wrong or doing it poorly that you don't do anything at all and "wait" upon the Lord.

Anxiety and fear are closely related, if not synonymous, in the creative process. Therefore dealing with anxiety is like dealing with fear: you must face it to overcome it. You must admit that you are anxious and identify the reasons why: fear of failure, fear of criticism, ignorance of how to start, not knowing how to finish. You must not hide behind the Lord and disguise your anxiety as something other than what it is.

At one time I had a proposal from my publisher to write a book on top of all the other writing and school work I am already doing. My anxiety told me not to do it; my thinking, however, told me I have done it before (write multiple projects) and can do it again, with God's help. What did I decide? It would have been nice for someone to step forward and give me a study/writing grant to cover my needs while I created and wrote. I decided to work on the book while pursuing my studies and continuing my consulting and speaking work. If I had not been studying anxiety, I'm not sure I would or could have made that decision.

How does the issue of anxiety apply to your creativity right now? What has you stuck in a non-productive or non-creative rut? I urge you to discover what it is and then get going on what you have talked about doing for a short or long time. Don't let anxiety rob you and the world any longer of the best you that you can be.

Too Late

I ran across a quote by Martin Luther King Jr. that impacted me deeply. Before I share that quote, however, I want to share a passage from Isaiah that people recite and even sing to me regularly (it was put to music years ago). It is their life philosophy and approach to missions, creativity and action, and it reads like this in the NAS Version:

> "He gives strength to the weary, And to him who lacks might He increases power. Though youths grow weary and tired, And vigorous young men stumble badly, ***Yet those who wait for the Lord*** Will gain new strength; They will mount up with wings like eagles, They will run and not get tired, They will walk and not become weary" (Isaiah 40:30-31 emphasis added).

A CLOSER LOOK

The key phrase in that passage for many is "those who wait on the Lord." The implication is that if you are going to serve the Lord, you need to wait. There is only one problem with that philosophy. Everything else in that passage speaks to action, not waiting. It speaks of strength, flying, running and walking. Those who are waiting aren't do any of those things, but the entire context of the passage is God giving strength to those who "wait." I would propose that those who wait don't need the strength.

The NIV for once is more accurate in its translation of the word "wait," for the NIV states, "but those who ***hope***

John W. Stanko

in the Lord will renew their strength." Insert that phrase back into the longer quote above, and you will see there is a big difference between hoping and waiting. Most already have the waiting down pat. I want to be one who hopes as I run, fly and walk, and I hope that we can run together toward our purpose and creativity.

THE QUOTE

And now for the quote from Martin Luther King's speech "Beyond Vietnam," delivered on April 4, 1967 in New York City. I will offer no commentary on his closing comments. I trust you to draw your own conclusions and make the necessary adjustments in your life and work to make room for what he said:

We are now faced with the fact, my friends, that tomorrow is today. We are confronted with the fierce urgency of now. In this unfolding conundrum of life and history, there is such a thing as being too late. Procrastination is still the thief of time. Life often leaves us standing bare, naked, and dejected with a lost opportunity. The tide in the affairs of men does not remain at flood - it ebbs. We may cry out desperately for time to pause in her passage, but time is adamant to every plea and rushes on. Over the bleached bones and jumbled residues of numerous civilizations are written the pathetic words, "Too late." There is an invisible book of life that faithfully records our vigilance or our neglect. Omar Khayyam is right: "The moving finger writes, and having writ moves on."

Time to Create

Have you wondered where creativity comes from? Have you also wondered why some people are more creative than others? For the most part, creativity continues to be a mystery to me. One thing I do know, however, and that is creativity is hard work! My writing does not descend from heaven, even if God inspires it (which I hope He does). I have to write and publish it. That's not glamorous or spiritual; it's just effort.

Many people tell me that they are more productive because they don't have enough time to write, paint, study, or think, for that matter. You know my response to that excuse: You have all the time there is in the world--24 hours every day. It's what you *do* with that time that will set you apart as a creative or non-creative person.

By now you know I am a big fan of Julia Cameron. In her book *The Sound of Paper: Starting from Scratch*, Cameron says this about the issue of time and creativity:

> Most of us think, "If only I had more time, then I would create." We have a fantasy that there is such a think as good creative time, an idyll of endless, seamless time unfolding invitingly for us to frolic in creativity. No such bolts of limitless time exist for most of us. Our days are chopped into segments, and if we are to be creative, we must learn to use the limited time that we have.
>
> When ego is siphoned of creativity, when

creativity becomes one more thing we do, like laundry, it takes far less time to do it. Much of our desire for creative time has to do with our trying to coax ourselves into being in the right mood to create. We want to "feel like it," and when we don't feel quickly, we think the solution is more time. Actually, the solution is less attention to the vagaries of mood. In short, creativity needs to become daily, doable and nonnegotiable; something as quotidian [everyday, commonplace, ordinary] as breathing. When we make a special occasion out of our art, we rob ourselves of the time we actually have.[8]

Often I don't start creating because I don't believe I have enough time to complete what I start. When that is the case, I need to trust that God will help me use the time I have. At other times, I don't start something because I am afraid I won't have enough time to do it *well*. When that happens, I need more courage, not more time. I need to begin and trust that what I don't consider "good enough" may be more than good enough to impact someone else. I can't let my perfectionism inhibit my ability to produce what I can, when I can, no matter how meager it may seem.

When I wrote my New Testament devotional, I sat down to write and somehow the creative process always kicked in, and the result was a large body of work of which I am quite pleased. As I edit this book, it is 9 PM on a Saturday night and I am in Guyana, South America. I am tired and have work to do to speak tomorrow, but I am driven to get this manuscript done. It's just grunt work at this point and I will trudge through to the end.

You have the time and you also have the creative ability. Now all you have to do is spend a little time every day bringing forth what has probably been in you for some time. You are a creative person; don't waste your creativity on excuses of why you can't produce. Move past your fears and invest some time and hard work. In the long run, you and the world will be the better for those efforts.

A Fat Duck

I found this quote a few years ago from Ralph Waldo Emerson: "Our chief want is someone who will inspire us to be what we know we could be." That is what I have tried to do through the Monday Memo and my purpose teaching: Inspire you to be who God created you to be, who you have always wanted to be creative. I have found, however, that some resemble the duck described by the philosopher Soren Kierkegaard. I hope you aren't like this duck, but just to make sure you aren't, you had better read on.

GROUNDED

The story has it that there was a duck flying with other wild ducks when they flew over some tame ducks in a barnyard. The wild duck decided to stay with these tame ducks for a while. He stayed for an hour, a day and then several months. Finally, his wild duck cohorts flew overhead one day and beckoned the wild duck to rejoin them, which he gladly did.

He found, however, that his barnyard living had made him so soft and heavy that he could not fly high enough to join his former mates. So he dropped back into the barnyard, promising that he would get in shape to join them the next time. The next time he heard them, he flapped his wings but could not even get off the ground. Finally, after many attempts, wishful thinking and a lot of broken promises, the wild duck became a domesticated bird that looked good but never went anywhere.

FLYING HIGH OR NOT AT ALL?

Did you dream of flying high at one time? Better yet, did you actually taste the heights you had determined to reach? Then where are you now? Are you still flying high or content with the safety and provision of the barnyard full of chickens and goats?

I am almost 65 years of age as I write and I still have a lot of flying I want to do. I now teach at the university at both the undergraduate and graduate level and will soon start teaching online classes. I continue to produce regular Bible studies that are regularly sent to thousands of people, as well as writing a daily devotional. I want to fly high and refuse to forsake the heights of productivity for the safety of the barnyard, with its regular rations. I listen to music that inspires me, go to places that move me and read books that engage me. I want to fly high and far and I do things that contribute to those objectives.

Flying high can be dangerous, but the view is fantastic! This week, ask yourself some tough questions. Do you talk about flying, or do you really fly? Are you content with barnyard chatter and routine, or are you ready to flap your wings to see how high and far you can go? I hope you are ready to fly and you will take others with you on the journey. I look forward to seeing you in high places. If you settle for the barnyard, we won't be meeting any time soon.

Creativity Tips and Strategies

All right, we have covered a theology of creativity, your role in creativity and the battle you must wage against fear if you are going to create. In this final Section, I include more tips and strategies beyond just battling fear – although I do address fear one more time. I assume by this time that you are ready to say you are creative and get about the work of expressing it. Here are some suggestions and role models I think will help you do just that.

Wisdom for Creativity

In previous sections, I urged you to read Proverbs 8 and study wisdom as a source of creative inspiration and direction. Let's look at another passage about wisdom from Proverbs 8:30-31: "Then I [wisdom] was constantly at his side. I was filled with delight day after day, rejoicing always in his presence, rejoicing in his whole world and delighting in mankind."

Wisdom was at God's side when He created the earth. Therefore if you want to be more creative, you need more wisdom. Wisdom in creativity is not always having a thought or idea that has never existed in the history of mankind. It is the ability to address new challenges and problems with a combination of new and existing knowledge.

Take bottled water, for example. The developers invented neither plastic nor water. They simply applied and combined existing entities to meet a need for portable drinking water. The equation for this was as follows: need + water + plastic bottle x wisdom = a billion dollar industry.

The implications of this concept to the application of wisdom and expression of creativity are important, for you have already applied this equation to your life on a regular basis. For example, you take time + tasks + experience = your daily schedule. Or even words + understanding of grammar + meaning + your unique perspective + your vocabulary combinations = speech. You are creative and express it every day. In fact, someone said that today you will string together words and utter a sentence that has probably never been spoken in the history of mankind as you will say it.

While creativity does not require totally new concepts, inventions or ideas (although it can), it will involve your unique perspective on life situations that you face every day. No one else on earth looks at life and its events as you do. When you address those things, you will do so in a way that no one else has ever done. If you think, however, that you are not creative, you will miss your chance to contribute something new to the ongoing expression of life as you know and see it here on earth. And you will simply tell others or at least think to yourself, "I am not creative" when you are a creative machine.

Are you ready to face, embrace and express your creativity? What you need is not creativity, but the wisdom to express your creativity and that you can have in abundance, but only if you have faith: "If any of you lacks wisdom, you should ask God, who gives generously to all without finding fault, and it will be given to you. But when you ask, you must believe and not doubt, because the one who doubts is like a wave of the sea, blown and tossed by the wind" (James 1:5-6). I encouraged you to stop running from or misunderstanding your creativity, but instead ask for wisdom as to how to express it as you walk through your life assignment.

Steve Jobs

I use a MacBook Pro computer, so I have been interested in the Apple company and Steve Jobs in particular. I read Walter Isaacson's book, *Steve Jobs*, and I learned a lot about creativity and how Steve Jobs approached the topic. Let's me share with you what I learned from Isaacson's authorized version of Jobs' life and work.

There was great debate after Jobs' passing as to whether or not he knew the Lord. From what I read, it doesn't seem like he did, but I will leave that in God's hands. Jobs was certainly impacted by Zen Buddhism and a host of other spiritual influences apart from Christianity, but no one can deny that he almost singlehandedly changed the world by expressing his creativity. While not a technology man, Jobs was a design and systems guy who was nothing short of brilliant in what he did, whether fashioning an iPad or crafting Apple, his beloved company.

Jobs by all accounts, including his own, however, was a difficult man, sometimes mean and demeaning. He had no tolerance for fools and, in his estimation, most people were fools. What can we learn from this man while not emulating his style, but certainly emulating his passion? Here are some things to think about:

1. You may be so afraid to offend or challenge others that you keep your ideas and thoughts carefully locked inside. The world then loses the best of what you have because you are afraid to speak and act.

2. Sometimes you are more afraid of success than failure. You don't try to have your first success because you are not sure you can sustain it.

3. You can take for granted what you see and what you can do. You may think everyone sees what is obvious to you, but often then don't. When you think like that, you don't say or do much. You don't make things happen, you watch things happen.

4. You may be afraid of mistakes and therefore choose to do "no" thing rather than do the wrong thing.

Steve Jobs did not allow any of these things to hinder him and he changed the world. I maintain that you and I, in partnership with God's Spirit, should be equally as creative as Jobs, while not necessarily playing to a world audience.

What is keeping you from being creative and expressing your creativity? My objective, however, is not just that you know what creativity is in theory but that you know so you can overcome your obstacles to run the creative race. I am personally challenged by Jobs' example, for if he did that for the glory of technology, what can or should I do for the glory of God? I pray you will join me in asking and answering the same question, and that together we can impact our world with the greatness of the image of God that still resides in you and me.

ABBA

I was in the UK a few years ago packing late at night (or early in the morning) to head home. I had the television on, and a documentary was showing about the music group ABBA. I was casually listening but it caught my attention when they talked about how hard they worked to create their music when they were at their peak. Since then, I have seen the musical *Mama Mia*, which incorporates ABBA's diverse music into a show about a confused young girl about to get married, and after that I became even more intrigued with ABBA's work.

The documentary is now on YouTube and it makes for interesting viewing, even if it is 89 minutes long! If you can't watch it all, pick it up at about the nine-minute mark through about minute twelve. This is not a post to promote ABBA's music, but I do want to commend their approach to creativity, for their approach was one of disciplined, hard work. In other words, their creative success was no fluke. They had the talent, but they worked their talent hard, taxing it to produce what it was intended to do.

I write every day. Then I write the Monday Memo once a week. I produce a new Bible study every two weeks and publish at least one book each year. Those projects happen because I sit down to do the work, and I am always preparing, taking notes and perfecting my craft. I teach new classes regularly and read and listen to books almost daily.

If you want to write, paint, sculpt, teach, or start a business or ministry, then you will need to do what I do, what ABBA did. You will need to work and apply yourself.

Now you don't *have* to do this, for when you force yourself, you will find all kinds of reasons not to create. You must *want* to do this, so you can face and conquer your fears. You will need to deal with the apathy or ambivalence of those around and even close to you. None of my books are considered "best sellers," but I will keep writing to perfect my skills. Maybe one day God will honor me with that kind of success. If not, I will keep writing - maybe it will happen after I'm gone. Maybe it will never happen.

I hope you are encouraged by this time to embrace and express your creativity in new, fresh ways. This will not just happen without your concerted, focused effort. If I can help you in any way, please let me know. Now get busy about the work you were created to create.

Weirdly Creative

What is weird creativity? I'm glad you asked. Weird creativity is so far outside the realm of normal, pretty much as far away as Pluto is from Earth. Yet weird creativity can become normal creativity if you aren't afraid of it when it first shows up. Let me explain.

WEIRD CREATIVITY

There was a movie out years ago called *Abraham Lincoln: Vampire Hunter*, based on a novel by a man named Seth Grahame-Smith. The film portrays Lincoln, the U.S. sixteenth president, as someone having a secret identity as a vampire hunter. The novel and film "rewrite" history to show that most of Lincoln's decisions as president were not based on politics but on his desire to destroy vampires.

That's weird creativity.

What happened to this weirdness? It is now a best-selling book and movie. Yes, it's up there in the weird hall of fame along with Andy Warhol's Campbell Soup can art, Edgar Allan Poe's morbid stories, the Hummer vehicle and Crocs shoes. Notice what each one of those things has in common: Each one is a commercial, if not spiritual or aesthetic, success.

Now ask yourself: How often have you had an idea, but dismissed it as "weird"? How often has someone produced something, only to have you say, "I had that idea years ago!" Why didn't you do anything about it? You thought it was weird, you thought you were weird, or you were afraid of the "weirdness" you would have to go through to make it happen.

YOU LOSE

You lost out on your creative expression because you set yourself up as judge and jury of what is weird and what isn't. In the process, you keep getting lapped in the creativity race by those who aren't thinking and are just doing something with their weirdness. You think, they do, you lose.

When you stop to think of it, almost all creativity is weird at first thought. How about bottled water, a phone you can carry with you anywhere, or a computer the size of a wrist watch (anyone remember the comic strip character Dick Tracy?).

Let's make a deal. Take some time this week and focus on an idea you have - the 'weirder' the better. Then spend two hours this week on making it happen, or at least taking a step toward making it happen. You can go to the library, research the Internet, write out a business plan, write the first chapter of the book or the first three poems of your anthology about growing up in Madagascar. Whatever your mind is telling you, "That's weird!" will be your focus for the week. Don't listen to anyone else tell you it's weird, just invest the time into making it a reality.

If a man can rewrite history to portray Abraham Lincoln as a vampire hunter, then what can you and I produce who are created in the image of God? Should we not be able to produce "weird" but uplifting stuff? I think we can, but first we have to surrender our desire to judge what's in our heart and take steps to make it happen.

Why We Write (or Create)

I thought I would look at the other side of the coin and list reasons why we do (or should) write. If you aren't a writer, substitute the word "create" for the word "write" and see if the reasons fit your life's situation. Here's the list:

1. Writing allows you to clarify your thinking and means to express it. Someone once said, "You write what you hear so you can see what you think." Makes sense to me. I am a better speaker because I write!

2. Writing helps provide a legacy, for your writings may out-survive you, God willing.

3. When you write, you can generate an audience over and over again every time someone picks up your book to read or passes it along to someone else.

4. When you write, you generate an audience far beyond those you can touch personally. Many of my books are published in other countries and are there when I cannot be.

5. You can make money from writing. I know I have. Sometimes you pray for money and God gives you an idea. You have to convert that idea into reality and then the money comes.

6. You honor what God does in your life by recording it to make it available to help or encourage others.

7. You write so you don't forget what the Lord has shown you or done in your life. An old saying says, "The problem with taking mental notes is the ink fades so quickly." Even writing a journal enhances your faith as you look back on your history with Him.

8. When you give yourself permission to create, you give the same permission to others.

9. Writing is a great means to influence others, which is the essence of godly leadership. Some want authority to lead; I choose influence and writing gives it to me.

10. When you create, you are functioning in one aspect of being created in the image of the Creator. He creates and gave the same capacity.

There you have my list. Did I miss any reasons that you can think of? If I did, send me an email and let me know any other reasons you have come up with. And remember, don't dismiss this list if you are not a writer. If you are sculptor, business consultant, poet, speaker or painter, go through the list and see if any of those reason are or can be motivation for you to create.

The Worst Conference in the History of the World

All right, I confess. I was going to leave this essay out, but I just had to get just one more lesson in about failure, including one in this Section about creativity tips and strategies. Perhaps you left the topic behind after Section Three, but here it is again. This time I want to share another one of my failures, which was spectacular—or at least in my mind it was. I am doing this with the hope that it will help you celebrate your own failures as I celebrate mine. Permit me to share just one more failure.

THE WORST CONFERENCE
IN THE HISTORY OF THE WORLD

When I was with a Christian music company I helped plan and organize the worst conference in the history of the world! Our team was going to Dallas about this time of year. We thought registrations were coming in slowly, but didn't think there was anything to worry about. Then we learned right before we were scheduled to be there that the postal service had lost all 50,000 of our brochures. Only a few were delivered and that explained the low response.

Instead of canceling the event, we pulled out all the stops to spread the word that we were coming, confident we could still have a successful event. Were we ever mistaken!

On the first night of the event, we had less than 1,000 people in a church that seated 5,000. Right after we started the event, the sound system failed. When I returned from trying to work in the audio booth, I saw the worship leader on stage playing the guitar and trying to lead worship. (This man wasn't known for his guitar-playing skills, believe me.) When he asked for the words to come up on the side screen, it was then we realized that the projection system had malfunctioned. The bulb burned out and the church didn't have a spare.

I ran backstage to try and print off some sheets with the words on them only to discover that the copy machine was broken. I got up to take an offering and apologized, saying that I felt like I should be paying anyone who happened to be there that evening. To make matters worse, the event went on to lose about $15,000. I realized that weekend that a bad event is like flushing a toilet. Once you flush, there isn't any way you can stop the process; you just have to let it run its course. That is how a badly planned event can be.

TWO CHOICES

I had two choices after that disastrous weekend. The first was to quit, which I briefly considered. The second was to take three months between Dallas and our next scheduled event and study what went wrong. I chose the latter and we went through everything we did. We came up with a number of innovations and built in more than a few safeguards to make sure what happened in Dallas would never happen again.

By God's grace, our next event was a fantastic success. We introduced some changes that generated quite a bit of revenue, and our team was better prepared and focused. Today I thank God for that terrible Dallas event and some others that followed. I learned more from those failures than

I ever did from the good events. I also learned that a bad event isn't the end of the world.

When a baseball player strikes out or a soccer player misses a wide open goal, they don't go off the field and sit in the stands. They keep playing through their failure. In practice, they work on their technique but in the game they keep swinging and kicking. That's what you and I need to do as well.

Don't let your failures discourage you. Don't give up on your dream. Accept that failure is a part of every successful person's life, even your own. Adjust your expectations, but don't quit! Today I can organize great events because I organized some poor ones.

I want to treat my failures like a good steak. I pay a lot of money for a good steak and I want to enjoy every morsel. The same is true for my failures. I have often paid a high price for them, and I want to gain all I can from my purchase. I want to chew, digest and process them as completely as possible. I also don't want to live through them again if I don't have to, so I want to learn so I don't duplicate them in the future. I invite you to join me as a fellow student of our failures so that we can graduate to school of success!

Climb Your Mountain

Did you ever feel like you were facing insurmountable odds as you work to be creative? Do you feel like you are facing an uphill climb to do God's will? If so, you are not alone. Not only are there plenty of people today who feel what you feel, there were some in the past who did as well.

One such person was Jonathan, Saul's son and David's friend. While everyone around him felt stifled by their obstacles and opposition, Jonathan decided to do something about it. His story is found in 1 Samuel 13:20-14:23. You may want to read those verses again before you proceed with the rest of this essay.

TWO CLIFFS WITH NAMES

It is interesting that Saul's army was pretending to fight when Jonathan decided to engage the enemy. The army daily went through the motions of fighting, yet they never did anything. That reminds me some creative "wannabes." They often go through maneuvers, but they don't really attack their real enemies of fear, laziness and lack of faith.

Once Jonathan decided to fight the Philistines, he faced formidable odds. There were only two of them (Jonathan and his armor bearer) against a whole Philistine army. They only had one sword between them, and they had to scale two large cliffs with names. A cliff has to be significant to have a name and both of these cliffs had them, so they must have been foreboding.

When Jonathan decided to climb up, the Lord didn't

carry Him in the "shadow of his wings." Jonathan had to climb using his hands and feet. Maybe he got dirt under his fingernails. His armor bearer probably even got a mouthful of dirt climbing behind Jonathan.

They made it to the top of the cliffs, however, and the Philistines were surprised to see them. They were so surprised that Jonathan and his sidekick had a serious competitive advantage, and that advantage was courage. What can you learn from this story of courageous action in the face of difficulty?

START CLIMBING!

Jonathan came to the right conclusion as he considered whether or not to climb his mountain. He voiced it when he said, "Come, let's go over to the outpost of those uncircumcised fellows. Perhaps the Lord will act in our behalf. Nothing can hinder the Lord from saving, whether by many or by few" (1 Samuel 14:6).

Jonathan didn't let his circumstances prevent him from taking action. He was looking for some sign, any sign to attack rather than any sign why he should not attack. Is your attitude the same as Jonathan's? Are you looking for any sign to indicate that you should take action and create? Or are you waiting for conditions to be just right before you take your first steps?

There is only one way to get on top of your situation and that is to climb up from where you are. You can't wish your cliffs away or blow them up. Nor can you conclude that mountains in your way are not God's will. Usually, they are. Climbing them will make your creativity and productivity more memorable and special.

Where can you apply the lessons of Jonathan and his armor bearer this week? What cliffs are you facing? When will you start climbing? What is at the top that is worth the climb? Jonathan succeeded one step at a time and

God helped him, even though He was greatly outnumbered. Rest assured that God will help you in the same way, but you must first start climbing and creating. Don't put it off another day. It's time to move on up to the high creative place that God has for you.

You Want Certainty

In the last essay, we looked at the story of Jonathan and his assistant and examined how they had to climb two cliffs to get to their desired goal. You have obstacles and cliffs to climb as well, and I urged you to start climbing.

There is one more question, however, that may be keeping your feet on the ground instead of on your cliffs heading upward. What is that question? I'm glad you asked! The question is: How do I know I am climbing the right cliff heading to the right destination, the right path for the correct goal?

The answer is you **don't** know. For the explanation, read on.

PERHAPS

We all want answers and assurance before we set out that we are on the right track. If that's what you want, you are not alone. This desire, however, can actually hinder more than help as you try to pursue goals and aspirations you have.

You need to see what Jonathan said to understand what I mean:

> Jonathan said to his young armor-bearer, "Come, let's go over to the outpost of those uncircumcised fellows. **Perhaps** the Lord will act in our behalf. Nothing can hinder the Lord from saving, whether by many or by few" (1 Samuel 14:6 emphasis added).

The key word that Jonathan uttered is **perphaps**. Jonathan knew there were no guarantees in what he was about to do. He had faith, but was his faith accurate? There was only one way to find out, and that was to start climbing. He knew God **could** deliver through just two of them, he just didn't know if God **would** deliver through the two of them.

There are some who see doubt as the enemy of faith; I rather see it as a part of the faith process. If you knew for sure, it wouldn't require faith, now would it? But what's to keep you from climbing wrong cliffs on a regular basis?

WHAT'S IN YOUR HEART?

The answer is found in what the assistant said to Jonathan when he heard of Jonathan's plan. He said: "Do all that you have in mind," his armor-bearer said. "Go ahead; I am with you heart and soul" (1 Samuel 14:7). Why can often trust what's in your mind and heart? You can because of how the Amplified Bible interprets Proverbs 16:4: "Roll your works upon the Lord [commit and trust them wholly to Him; **He will cause your thoughts to become agreeable to His will**, and] so shall your plans be established and succeed" (emphasis added).

Do you have any good ideas? Is there something that's been in your heart to do for a while? If so, then start climbing. **Perhaps** the Lord will help you. What if He doesn't? Try again, this time climbing a different cliff. The point is that you want answers **before** you go and the Lord will provide answers **as** you go.

I urge you to follow in the footsteps of Jonathan and his aide. Get moving and stop worrying about the results. God is with you, even if you have to retrace some of your steps. As you go, you will get a better view from a higher vantage point and it will only help to make your journey, perhaps even your PurposeQuest, a more scenic and memorable one.

Creative Collaboration

Every year I highlight Christmas music on my Saturday radio show. Many of the men who wrote the carols of old were theologians who had a deep grasp on the significance of Jesus' birth. If you go past the first verse of some carols, you hear some magnificent truths about Jesus and the implications for mankind of His coming. One of my favorite hymns is *Hark the Herald Angels Sing*, which will be featured in one of my two shows.

WHO WROTE IT?

All credit for *Hark the Herald Angels Sing* is usually attributed to Charles Wesley, the brother of Methodism's founder, John Wesley. Charles was a prolific song writer, with almost 9,000 hymns to his credit. Charles only employed sombre, slow and solemn music for his lyrics, however, so this particular carol was sung to a tune other than we know for at least 100 years after it was written in 1739.

In 1840, a man named Felix Mendelssohn wrote a commemorative cantata to honor Johann Gutenberg's invention of the printing press. What does that have to do with this carol? Nothing except that a man named William Cummings heard the cantata and felt one of the melodies could better serve the magnificent lyrics Wesley had penned for *Hark the Herald*. Cummings adapted Mendelssohn's melody to Wesley's lyrics and the result was the version of *Hark the Herald Angels Sing!* we know today. So *Hark the Herald* is the result of a century-long creative collaboration by three men who never met over a period of 100 years!

CHRISTMAS CREATIVITY

This strikes me as a classic example of the simplicity and interconnection of the creative process. Your creativity doesn't have to involve something completely new or original. Cummings took two existing things - Mendelssohn's music and Wesley's words - to create something new again. He improved something that already existed to create something fresh that has impacted the world for more than a century.

I am planning my creative expressions for the future, which include a Purpose Bible, my next book, a new daily devotional, and starting a publishing company. I am a creative person, and so are you! The ideas you have can change the world, if you will stop discounting them as meaningless or insignificant. You don't have to invent something totally new to qualify as creative; you just have to act on your ideas and release them to the world. With God as your agent, the world will then act to endorse the very creativity that you may be dismissing or taking for granted.

Do you have any good ideas, even if they are only to improve something that already exists? If you do, take heart and remember Wesley, Mendelssohn and Cummings. Those three men who never met collaborated to create something memorable. There is no reason why you and I can't do the same thing.

More Media

For many years, I have felt that more media was in my future. When I put on the headphones, I sense God's presence and pleasure. I would have great interviews, and hosts would say, "I am going to have you back." In most cases, they never did. It was always a mystery why that would happen.

In 2008, I had a windfall profit from a trip to England, and decided to invest it in internet radio to both learn and reach more people with the purpose message. It was a great experience. I did 13 shows, had 1,000 listeners a show and 30 people downloaded a show to listen to every day. But when I ran out of money, I stopped the show to wait for another time. Last year was that time for the internet, and the response has been good. I have had a blast.

Today I host three Internet shows and two shows on local AM stations. On all the shows I interview others because I figure since no one ever did it for me, I should try to do it for someone else—and the "it" is allowing people to tell their purpose or creative story. I have found most people eager to tell it, and I want to give them their chance.

Furthermore, I just agreed to produce 13 television segments of a show called *Your PurposeQuest* that will air on a local cable channel. After they air on that channel, I have free access to post them online. I am excited to be able to develop that show and the supportive material to go with it. Some friends and I have many exciting, creative ideas to incorporate into that endeavor.

All in all, it's an exciting time. Yet it's not about me,

it's about the message God gave me, the message of purpose that continues to impact people all over the world. Don't ask me how, but I feel there is even more media in my future; I just can't see it all yet - but I can see me doing it.

Who knows, maybe one day a show will be live in your city via syndication! Now that would be a grand thing, and I will work toward developing material and a show worthy of such exposure. How, what can you do this week that will bring you a step closer to a dream you have? It doesn't have to media; it just has to be in your heart. Stop waiting for someone to invite you to the dance; invite yourself. Or as Seth Godin says, start your own parade. When you do, there's no telling who will join your procession or how many lives you will touch.

An Audience of One

I am not alone in what I do on Sunday nights. There is another memo going out that is known by the name *The Monday Morning Memo*. Written by Roy Williams, it is an update that focuses on branding, ad copy and creativity. I recommend it along with Williams' book entitled *The Wizard of Ads*. Both contain tools that can help sharpen and focus your creativity. One time Williams wrote a *Monday Morning Memo* that I want to summarize for you this week.

AHEAD OF THEIR TIMES

First Williams quoted Peter Drucker, the late management guru, who pointed out that business schools today are studying books that were poorly received at first and didn't sell well. Williams concluded that the loneliest people can often be those who create ahead of their times.

This led to a discussion of Ludwig von Beethoven, who basically gave up on his ability to please and compose for his generation. Instead he composed for a "later age" because so many of his contemporaries criticized and ignored his work!

> "When a true genius appears in this world, you may know him by this sign, that the dunces are all in confederacy against him"—Jonathan Swift, author of *Gulliver's Travels*.

> "Great spirits often encounter violent opposition from mediocre minds"—Albert Einstein.

"Funeral by funeral, science makes progress"
—Paul Samuelson.

"Yes, even scientists ahead of their times are rejected by their peers," added Williams.

AN AUDIENCE OF ONE

Emily Dickinson wrote with complete confidence that her words would never be read. When she died, her family found 1,700 of her poems in a drawer. Many of these poems rank with the greatest ever written, but were never read by anyone while she was alive. Perhaps she was being prophetic when she wrote:

Fame is a fickle food upon a shifting plate,

Whose table once a Guest, but not the second time is set.

Whose crumbs the crows inspect, and with ironic caw

Flap past it to the Farmer's corn; Men eat of it and die.

Williams concluded *The Memo* with: "Dickinson wrote for herself, an audience of one. Study the lives of the Great Ones and you'll find this to be a common characteristic among them."[9]

The application for you is simple. Do you have something new and different to say or do? Are you willing to write or perform for an audience of one? If so, then get busy this week being true to who you are and don't pay attention to what others think or say. Just do it. I read once that Beethoven stopped producing music for his generation because his work was so poorly received. He started composing music for the next generation and today his work is known the world over.

Perhaps you are a creative pioneer, a possibility I am considering as I study the sales results of my books. I write in faith that if my books are not popular now, they could be after I am gone. Either way—whether God blesses now, later, or not at all—I will continue to produce what I see and feel and hope for the best. In the meantime, I don't mind writing for an audience of one, especially if that audience is the Lord Himself.

Balance is Bunk

I was adding up the numbers the other day, and discovered that I've met with almost 3,500 people in the last twelve years to talk one-on-one about purpose. That's almost one person every day for five years! One thing's for sure: Those numbers give me a unique perspective on purpose and the challenges people face in finding and fulfilling it. There is one phrase that I hear all the time when I meet with people. Perhaps I would hear you say it if got together. What is the phrase? I'm glad you asked. That phrase is a simple two words.

YES, BUT...

I hear "yes, but" all the time. Do you hate your job? "Yes, but I can't quit." Are you good at what you do? "Yes, but it's not me, it's the Lord." Do you want to travel? "Yes, but I'm not sure it's God's will." Do you want to be in ministry full-time? "Yes, but I'm not sure if it's the right time or season." Are you ready to do God's will in your life no matter what the cost? "Yes, but I want balance and don't want to go overboard on any one thing."

I have come to the conclusion that "yes, but" people are expert excuse makers. They use their magnificent creativity to concoct all kinds of reasons why now is not the time for them to produce, shine or make an impact. I have come to the conclusion that "yes, but" is really the same answer as "no." "Yes, but" sounds a whole lot better.

BALANCE IS BUNK

Many people stop short of effectiveness because they don't want to go overboard. They want to be balanced. They want to have faith, but not excessive faith. They want to address racism, for example, but not make anyone unhappy or uncomfortable. They want to see world-class results in their life, but not have to pay a world-class price.

I challenge you to name just one person who was balanced and made a difference in the world. Was Martin Luther or Martin Luther King? How about Nelson Mandela or Florence Nightingale? Perhaps Winston Churchill or Billy Graham?

Now you would say that those were great people who had a unique purpose to fulfill. All right then, think of your favorite teacher when you were growing up. Were they balanced or were they passionate about teaching and learning? Think of your favorite athlete or singer? How did they achieve that special place in your mind? They did it, I would guess, because they were completely committed to their craft or creativity. I would further imagine that they were not "yes, but" people, but "yes, and here's how we will do it" people.

Yes, I believe that balance is bunk, a myth that we pursue in our minds, a phantom that doesn't exist. The pursuit of balance makes us ineffective and at times boring. Listen to yourself this week and see if you are in the habit of saying, "Yes, but." If you are, then keep the yes, and get rid of the "but." From there, I urge you to get busy giving the world what you have that it needs. And don't worry about being balanced, for balance is certainly, most definitely and positively, **bunk**!

Bluegrass Special

In the previous essay, I wrote about balance. Basically, I'm against it. No, that's not completely accurate. I just don't think it's possible to be "balanced" and impact the world at the same time. I know some people disagree with me on this, especially people who were hurt by loved ones who abandoned them to pursue their passion.

I saw something recently that convinced me even more that balance and productivity, balance and purpose, balance and creativity are all mutually exclusive. What did I see? I'm glad you asked.

BLUEGRASS SPECIAL

I was channel flipping and came to a public television station that was showing a concert featuring Rhonda Vincent and The Rage from St. Louis. I had never heard of Rhonda or her group, but her voice caught my attention, so I decided to watch for a while. It turns out that Rhonda and The Rage are a bluegrass music group. For those outside of the U.S., bluegrass is a version of country western music. That's probably not the most accurate definition, but it will do for our purposes.

The Rage featured a violin, viola, mandolin, cello, upright bass fiddle, banjo, guitar and Rhonda's fantastic voice. When I went to their website, I found out that Rhonda has been voted outstanding female singer by the International Bluegrass Music Association for the last seven consecutive years. I remembered some of the songs from the television show and downloaded them through iTunes, that's how good I thought they were.

"So what," you may be asking? "John Stanko is into bluegrass music now, big deal." No, I'm not into bluegrass music but I sure got into reading about Rhonda Vincent. You know what I found out? Rhonda Vincent isn't balanced! In my opinion, that's the key to her phenomenal success in the world of bluegrass music.

ON THE ROAD AGAIN

I counted the concerts that Rhonda has in October and November and came up with 22. She is taking the month of December off, but then has 19 concerts in January and February. Her site lists concerts through next November. I think 41 concerts in five months is a lot of concerts, don't you? I wonder if she travels with her family, because I did see that she was wearing a wedding ring? Does she have children? I was unable to find out.

I know that Rhonda writes music and does a lot of recording, too. Ms. Vincent it totally committed to her love, her passion. That is who she is and she has impacted her world of influence like no other woman has ever done.

If that is what one woman can do in her chosen endeavor, what can you do? I'll tell you one thing: You won't do much if you choose to pursue balance. Balance is boring; passion changes lives. Balance causes you to be mediocre at doing a few things; passion drives you to be the best at one thing. You say, "I can do my best when I do a little work, a little family time, and a little ministry time." I say focus on one at a time and devote yourself to being the best you can be, whether it's being a parent, worker or pastor.

Was Paul balanced? Were Peter, James and John? How about Nelson Mandela, Martin Luther, Ernest Hemingway, or Beethoven? We know who those people are because they were passionate and they pursued what they did best. The world is in desperate need of who you are and what you have to offer. Please don't hide behind the balance myth; let your flame burn brightly and intensely for as many as possible to see. As you do, I know that you will take your place with the Rhonda Vincents of the world, who have decided to make their mark by being the best they can possibly be in their chosen vocation.

Conclusion

Whether you read this book straight through or took your time reading each Section, perhaps even over the last year, I hope you are now ready to create. This book is not your last venture into examining your creativity and many obstacles lie ahead as you seek to write, sculpt, speak, rhyme, do business, parent or do ministry. I know I will write more on creativity from time to time through my blog or The Monday Memo, so I urge you to follow me on either of those two free online programs. You can subscribe for either through my website, www.purposequest.com. I would also love to hear from you as to how this book helped you be more creative or any insights you may have on your creative journey. You can always write me at johnstanko@gmail.com. You never know when your insight may be included in one of my articles that will help others.

I am excited about what lies ahead for you as you create. There has never been a better day to produce creative projects and have them touch a broad international audience. I think the best is yet to come and I know that your creativity has the potential to impact the world, but only if you express it. Have faith, trust that God is with you and be ready for an exciting, fun-filled journey as you see to do God's will by accepting the fact that you are creative – and then working to see it expressed as only you can do with His help. Thank you and have fun!

Endnotes

[1] Julia Cameron, *The Right to Write* (New York: Jeremy P. Tarcher/Putnam, 1998), pages 100-101.

[2] Matthew Fox, *Creativity* (New York: Jeremy P. Tarcher/Penguin, 2002), page 77.

[3] Seth Godin, *Micro Marketing and the Called Bluff,* June 15, 2014.

[4] Parker Palmer, *The Active Life* (San Francisco: Jossey-Bass, 1999), page 31-32.

[5] Thomas Merton, *The Seeds of Contemplation* (New Directions, 2007), Kindle ebook, page 116.

[6] Eric Maisel, PhD, *The Van Gogh Blues: The Creative Person's Path through Depression* (Novato, California: New World Library, 2002), pages 101-102.

[7] Eric Maisel, PhD, *The Van Gogh Blues: The Creative Person's Path through Depression* (Novato, California: New World Library, 2002), page 104.

[8] Julia Cameron, *The Sound of Paper: Starting from Scratch* (New York: Jeremy P. Tarcher/Penguin, 2004), page 105.

[9] Roy H. Williams, *The Monday Morning Memo: The Lonely Outsider, published December 26, 2005, http://www.monday-morningmemo.com/newsletters/lonely-outsider/*

Creative Expressions

In an effort to stimulate creativity, I've collected a list of creative expressions common to our life experience. As you read the list, you may think, "Wait a minute! This list includes many of life's activities." If you had that thought, I would agree with you, and that's exactly the point I'm trying to make: Your life is filled with creative expressions. You may think, "I'm not very creative," but if think like that, you are incorrect. A creative God created you to be creative and you *will* be creative whether you think about it or not.

This understanding came to me recently as I adjusted my purpose statement to read "to **create** order out of chaos." Previously, I had presented my statement as "to **bring** order out of chaos." There is a big difference, however, between bringing and creating. This simple change has revolutionized how I view myself. Instead of seeing creativity as someplace I only "visited" on occasion, I now see myself as "living" there. I studied my life and saw that I am creative in what I do, not sometimes, but most of the time. Consider these personal expressions of my creativity:

1. Starting my businesses
2. Writing *The Monday Memo*
3. Writing my weekly Bible studies
4. Writing for my blog site
5. Consulting
6. Executive and leadership coaching
7. Developing and teaching seminars
8. My sense of humor

9. Writing books
10. Responding to emails
11. Event planning (As a Certified Meeting Professional)
12. Time management and organization
13. Travel arrangements and planning
14. Public speaking
15. Interviews on radio and television shows
16. Developing my website

As you review the creative expressions listed above and below, I don't want you to be content with studying someone else's lists. I want you to develop your own list of your personal creative expressions. If there are any that aren't on this list, please send them to me at johnstanko@ gmail.com and I will add them to my website list. Most importantly, use this list to stimulate your own creativity to recognize your creativity. You are creative!

So, without further ado, let's list the possible creative expressions that are common to the human experience:

1. Raising children
2. Handwriting
3. Wardrobe planning
4. Making repairs
5. Gardening and farming
6. Time management
7. Problem-solving
8. Cooking and baking
9. Decorating
10. Prayer
11. Gift-giving
12. Hospitality
13. Teaching
14. Song-writing
15. Editing
16. Organizing parties
17. Investing

18. Conducting war
19. Organization and structure
20. Building
21. Architectural design
22. Research
23. Arts and crafts
24. Sewing
25. Dance
26. Singing
27. Playing an instrument
28. Home-making
29. Drama and acting
30. Inventions
31. Poetry
32. Writing
33. Song arranging
34. Driving a vehicle
35. Choreography
36. Consulting
37. Movie making
38. Movie directing and producing
39. Acting
40. Humor
41. Playing and coaching sports
42. Photography
43. Painting and drawing
44. Sculpture
45. Leadership
46. Running a business
47. Daydreaming
48. Inventions and innovations
49. Advertising and public relations
50. Graphic design
51. Secretarial work
52. Hobbies, such as scrapbooking, stamp collecting, etc.
53. Thinking and daydreaming

54. Cosmetology and makeup
55. Menu planning
56. Thinking and daydreaming
57. Interior design
58. Landscape design
59. Computer programming
60. Website design
61. Goal-setting
62. Brainstorming
63. Team building
64. Linguistics
65. Product and package design
66. Surgery
67. Sales
68. Mentoring others
69. Meditating
70. Making excuses
71. Sin
72. Being the person you were never meant to be.

In addition, one reader was kind enough to send me these thoughtful considerations:

1. We create harmony and peace or discord and disruption through our chosen attitudes and responses to daily life.
2. When we choose to walk in the Spirit and be led by Him we have a hand in the creation of the fruits of the Spirit in our lives.
3. By stepping out in faith we create a spiritual space/ right atmosphere for God to work in.
4. We also create pleasure when we step out in faith - God's pleasure (without faith it is impossible to please Him).
5. When we exhort and encourage one another we help create in each other the strength and courage to persevere.

Another reader from Zimbabwe sent me the following excerpt:

> [Caroline] was not imaginative. She loved beauty and she was creative, but her creativeness found its joy in the shaping of everyday life to a form of comeliness, so that it became not just something that one put up with, but something that was enjoyable and lovely in itself. [Her brother] would have roared with derisive laughter if she had told him that making beds and baking cakes were activities that had for her beautiful shapes like flowers, but he snored in a well-made bed and devoured a well-made cake with equal pleasure and enthusiasm. - Elizabeth Goudge, "The Heart of the Family" (Hodder and Stoughton, Great Britain: 1953) p 134 .

Many people who make life beautiful and happy for others each day don't seem to see themselves as creative. To me this is sad, because we need these people even more than the great artists and musicians. They shape the whole world experience for the children and adults for whom they care and love. Selfless love is perhaps the most creative gift of all because it enables souls to blossom, and gives them the courage and confidence to reach out for their own creativity and place in the sun.

ABOUT THE AUTHOR

John Stanko was born in Pittsburgh, Pennsylvania. After graduating from St. Basil's Prep School in Stamford, Connecticut, he attended Duquesne University where he received his bachelor's and master's degrees in economics in 1972 and 1974 respectively.

Since then, John has served as an administrator, teacher, consultant, author, and pastor in his professional career. He holds a second master's degree in pastoral ministries, and earned his doctorate in pastoral ministries from Liberty Theological Seminary in Houston, Texas in 1995. He recently completed a second doctor of ministry degree at Reformed Presbyterian Theological Seminary in Pittsburgh.

John has taught extensively on the topics of time management, life purpose and organization, and has conducted leadership and purpose training sessions throughout the United States and in 32 countries. He is also certified to administer the DISC and other related personality assessments as well as the Natural Church Development profile for churches. In 2006, he earned the privilege to facilitate for The Pacific Institute of Seattle, a leadership and personal development program, and for The Leadership Circle, a provider of cultural and executive 360-degree profiles. He has authored fifteen books and written for many publications around the world.

John founded a personal and leadership development company, called PurposeQuest, in 2001 and today travels the world to speak, consult and inspire leaders and people everywhere. From 2001-2008, he spent six months a year in Africa and still enjoys visiting and working on that continent, while teaching for Geneva College's Masters of Organizational Leadership and the Center for Urban Biblical Ministry in his hometown of Pittsburgh, Pennsylvania. John has been married for 38 years to Kathryn Scimone Stanko, and they have two adult children. In 2009, John was appointed the administrative pastor for discipleship at Allegheny Center Alliance Church on the North Side of Pittsburgh where he served for five years. Most recently, John founded Urban Press, a publishing service designed to tell stories of the city, from the city and to the city.

You can stay in touch with John's world through the following sites and radio shows:

www.purposequest.com

www.johnstanko.us

www.stankobiblestudy.com

www.stankomondaymemo.com

www.blogtalkradio.com/acacthreads

www.blogtalkradio.com/genevacollegemsol

or via email at johnstanko@gmail.com

John also does extensive relief and community development work in Kenya. You can see some of his projects at www.purposequest.com/contributions

PurposeQuest International
PO Box 8882
Pittsburgh, PA 15221-0882

Additional Titles By John W. Stanko

A Daily Taste of Proverbs

A Daily Dose of Proverbs

What Would Jesus Ask You Today?

The Price of Leadership

Changing the Way We Do Church

Unlocking the Power of Your Purpose

Beyond Purpose

Life Is A Gold Mine: Can You Dig It?